A Life of Olson
& a Sequence of Glyphs on Points of his life, work, and times

Ed Sanders

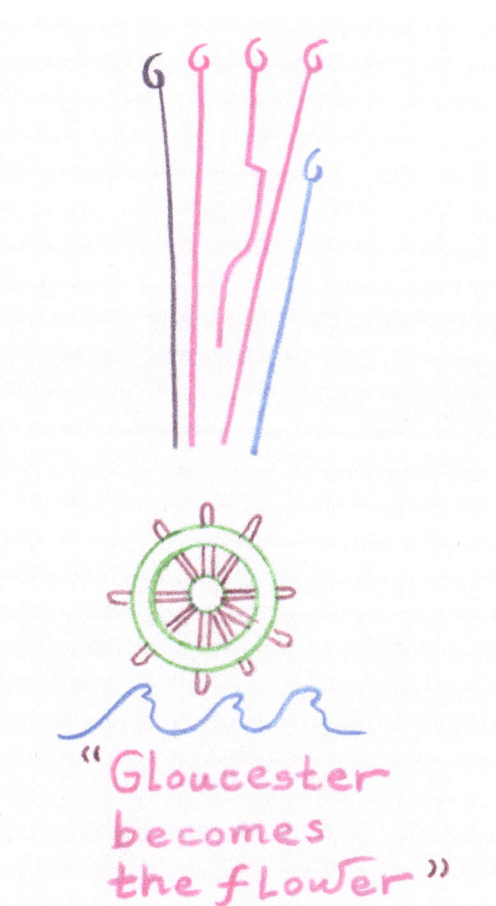

Copyright © 2018-2020 Ed Sanders

An expanded version of an illustrated lecture on the life and work of Charles Olson given at the Cape Ann Museum for the Gloucester Writers Center, October 27, 2018

© 2020 Ed Sanders
ISBN 978-1-949966-95-4 pbk. | ISBN 978-1-952419-28-7 hdc.

Library of Congress Cataloging-in-Publication Data

Names: Sanders, Ed, author.
Title: A life of Olson : & a sequence of glyphs on points of his life,
   work, and times / Ed Sanders.
Description: New York City : Spuyten Duyvil, [2020] |
Identifiers: LCCN 2020024203 | ISBN 9781949966954 (paperback) | ISBN
   9781952419287 (hardcover)
Subjects: LCSH: Olson, Charles, 1910-1970. | Poets, American--20th
   century--Biography.
Classification: LCC PS3529.L655 Z845 2020 | DDC 811/.54 [B]--dc23
LC record available at https://lccn.loc.gov/2020024203

On "A Life of Olson in Text and Glyphs"

I realize of course that Charles Olson's life and works are a limitless study but here is a Flow of Texts and Glyphs on his life, work, and era, including times when our lives intersected

I utilize what I call Glyphs extensively in this Life— color drawings combining images and text, which trace key points in the life of this amazing poet who wrote The Maximus Poems, and a sequence of historic texts which starred American & Personal History, & particularly the polis, or the city called Gloucester, "the flower" as he described it.

Just as Allen Ginsberg once wrote to one of his professors at Columbia, that Walt Whitman was a "Mountain too vast to be seen," so too Charles Olson always seemed to me to be almost a "Mountain too vast to be seen." Olson's life was so various and complicated that we can only stitch together a brief gathering of what we judge to be key points.

Again, he's a Mountain of Poetry, a Mountain of a Life, and a Mountain of someone to study!

I'm grateful to the Gloucester Writers Center, and to the Cape Ann Museum for the opportunity to present "A Life of Olson" as an illustrated talk, and also grateful to Michael Boughn and Kent Johnson of Dispatches, and T. Thilleman of Spuyten Duyvil for the publication of this book.

Ed Sanders

A Life of Olson
& a Sequence of Glyphs on Points
of his life, work, and times

    Such a bewildering sequence
        of interesting points
             in Olson's life!

    that I'm only able, for now,
    to "Glyphize"
        such a few!

    for the O(lson)keanos
        is Vast!

Born December 27, 1910
        in Worcester, Mass
            father Karl Joseph O
                mother Mary Hines O
    father born in Sweden
        mother born in Worcester of Irishness

Worcester Worcester
    you could take a trolley those days from W
                to Boston

Charles John Olson
    baptized as a Catholic

O grew up   in a 3rd-story flat
at 4 Norman Avenue
    heated by a coal stove

When O was 5
he went w/ his family
        during the summer
      to Gloucester
    for the 1st time
    at a camp cottage

    near Stage Fort Park

To Abbot Street Grammar school
    in Worcester '17-'24

    shoots up to six feet, seven inches!

1924-'28
    Classical High School in Worcester
    graduating with honors
        pres of his class
            captain of debating squad

1928
    wins the New England regional oratorical contest
        and third place in the national contest in D.C.

    his prize: a 10-week tour of Europe

1928-'32
    English major at Wesleyan U, Middletown, Conn
    on the debating team
        writes for Wesleyan newspaper
        goalie for soccer team
        candidate for Rhodes scholarship
            during his senior year

1929-'34
    comes back to Gloucester summertimes
        performs with several summer stock theaters
    works as substitute letter carrier (1931; his father
        Karl is a postman, and very involved in union activities)

Olson Sleuthing to Locate Herman Melville's Dispersed Personal Library
1932-1934

Olson attended Wesleyan
Working on his Master's Degree
in '32-'33
- height of the Depression

His thesis on Melville
was due on 5-1-'33

The fall of '32 he set out to locate
books once possessed
by H.M.

He sought most passionately
for the "Lost 500"
- those books M.'s wife had sold
to a dealer in Brooklyn in 1892 -

O traveled many locations
from NYC, Brooklyn, Pittsfield
& South Yarmouth, Mass
& in libraries
till by June of '34 he'd located 134 tomes
owned/used/read by H.M.
- some he'd annotated & marked
including a 7-volume Shakespeare
w/ M.'s notes on King Lear.

Olson transcribed onto 5x7 cards the publishing info
as well as the text & page #'s
of Melville's notes & reading marks

Melville's Book Boat

Sought out by Charles Olson

Sappho's Book Boat Song

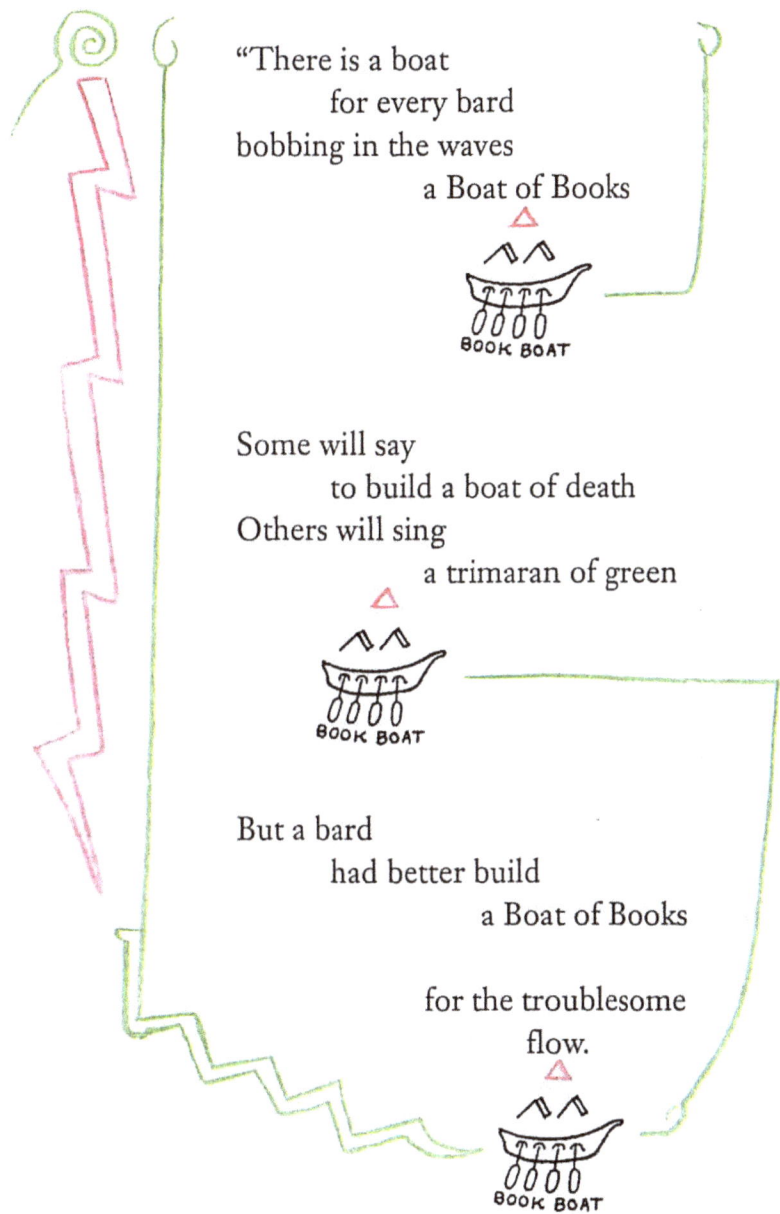

"There is a boat
      for every bard
bobbing in the waves
          a Boat of Books

Some will say
      to build a boat of death
Others will sing
         a trimaran of green

But a bard
     had better build
          a Boat of Books

        for the troublesome
         flow.

Olson Lauded in Matthiessen's 1941 Tome

Olson was lauded
in this famous book of 1941
      by F. O. Matthiessen

for his researches
into Melville's jottings
    in the various books
        of his personal library
especially in his 7-volume Shakespeare

which O travelled far and wide to locate
                and transcribe

Matthiessen praising Olson's 1937 essay, "Lear and Moby-Dick"

1934
    O obtains Olin Fellowship in Economics
        to continue reconstructing Melville's library
    In the fall starts teaching at Clark U in Worcester
    Delivers lecture on M's library in Pittsfield

1935
    O's father Karl passes August 31, at 53, of a cerebral hemorrhage
        in Worcester; his mother Mary
                moves to Gloucester

    He taught another year at Clark
    & on November 13 addressed an anti-war rally at the university

        described in the newspaper: "Probably the outstanding
        contribution of the day was
        the speech delivered by Professor
        Charles Olson, in which he
        pointed out the inherent
        barbarism in man, the emotional forces
        that drive men into battle— ending
        with the warning that only by
            substituting a cause with as great
        an appeal as war, only by fighting war
        with the fanaticism
            of religious maniacs,
                could the peacemakers
                    hope to avert war
                        even temporarily"

    It was an early estimation of his estimation
        of the human condition

    —to be reinforced in the '40s by his viewing
    of Corrado Cagli's drawings from Buchenwald
    & his learnng of the cannibalism
            on the whaling ship *Essex*
    & the bombing of Hiroshima & Nagasaki

        and as he proposed to me in a November 1965 letter,
        "a true Cruesade"...:

"I would <u>think</u> therefore that the only <u>Interesting</u>
political shot now possible, and sufficiently <u>meaningful</u>
would be something as mad as the Children's
(or Edward the Hermit's or Raymond of
Bourgogne

What in fact <u>is</u>
"JERUSALEM" ?

    Charles Olson, November 20,
      (1965)

1936
  met writer Edward Dahlberg, in Gloucester

    Sept, to Harvard University
      grad student in English
      & as teaching assistant to
        William Sedgwick

December, in NYC Dahlberg introduced Olson
        to Alfred Stieglitz

1937
completes a paper on Melville and Shakespeare
      for F. O. Mathiessen
    Sept, returns to Harvard
      as a Ph.D. candidate in the
        American Civilization program

  1938
    O's first trip to the West in July
      hitch-hiking K.C. to Seattle and S.F.
        takes bus back East

    Fall, continues at Harvard

  1939
    March, Guggenheim Fellowship for studies in Melville

1940
writes his initial poems
    May, in Gloucester meets Constance Wilcock

Oct '40-Apr '41
    lives on Christopher St. in Greenwich Village

May-June '41
    works two months for the
        American Civil Liberties Union
            as director of publicity

Bound for Glory
early 1942

Pete Seeger invited Charles Olson
to dine at the communal folk-singer pad
    called Almanac House
        in Greenwich Village

where Seeger showed Olson
some writings by Woody Guthrie

Olson asked Guthrie to write an article
for the magazine *Common Ground*
    (edited by Louis Adamic)

The result was a piece called "Ear Players"
which splashed quite brightly
    in the NY City intellectual waters

It was read, for instance, by an editor at E.P. Dutton
    named William Doerflinger
    who commissioned
    the book which became Guthrie's
        Bound for Glory

1942 September
>begins work for the Office of War Information
in D.C. Becomes the Associate Chief, Foreign
Language Division

1943
Olson & Connie Wilcock rent an apartment
on Randolph Place N.E., in D.C.

Collaborating with artist Ben Shahn
O creates a 24-page pamphlet,
"Spanish Speaking Americans in the War:
the Southwest"

his only publication for the government.

May 1944
Olson resigns from the Office of War Information
to protest the censorship

July he works for the Democratic National Committee
first at the National Convention in Chicago

Roosevelt & Truman
July 19, 1944

Roosevelt came in his private train to Chicago
for the Democratic Convention

Big time pols are a bit like wolves
& I think the Dem-wolves
felt FDR soon would pass
& that the VP would be the president

so it was grrrr
get Wallace
out of here
grrrr

Senator Harry Truman of Missouri looked good to them
though some wanted Supreme Court Justice William O. Douglas
& James Byrnes (later Truman's secretary of state)
truly hungered for it
Wallace had a lead on the first ballot

        but Truman swept into place
                      on the second

          setting the stage for the dropping of the a-bomb

O went to the 1944 Democratic Convention in Chi
   keeping his fingers crossed that Wallace
               would beat out Truman for vp

Toward the campaign's close
   O organized a salute to FDR
               at Madison Square Garden

Everybody for Roosevelt
November 1944

After Olson resigned
from the Office of War Information,
he worked for a while
    for the Democratic National Committee.

One of his duties
was organizing
    an "Everybody for Roosevelt" rally
  at Madison Square Garden
      just before the Election

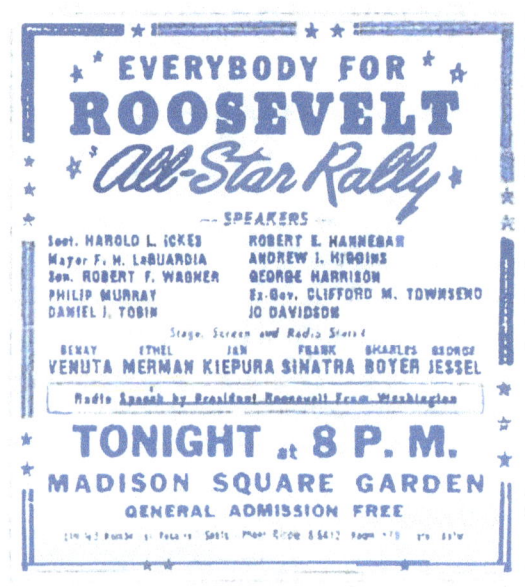

O made sure the entertainers
including George Jessel, Frank Sinatra
    & Ethel Merman
were comfortable back stage —

He stood in the spotlight
to introduce
    Sinatra

Ed Sanden
February 19, 2018

First Reading of Pound

Connie & Charles
went to Key West in early '45
where they resided in the
    bungalo of the Hemingway House
So that O wrote daily
        at Ernest's own desk
at which, for example, he'd written
    "For Whom the Bell Tolls"
& with Ernest's book collection
        still on the shelves —
O pulled down Hemingway's
        copy of Pound's "Personae"
— his 1st reading of Pound
    who was very much in the news
    returning from Italy
        & accused of treason

Edward Sanders
February 20, 2018

Leaving Politics

Early '45 he created a Poem initially called "The Telegram"
later changed to "The K"
      marking
his departure from politics
              for writing

Among the Sequence of Early Greatness:

      The K
      early '45

      Trinacria
      2-46

      The Moebius Strip
      by 9-46

In Praise of the Fool or The Green Man
      9-46

      La Préface
      9-46

      The Kingfishers
      7-20-49
with its famous opening line:
"What does not change / is the will to change"

Early Olson

1940s D.C.

(Kate Olson archive)

Finishing Call Me Ishmael
1945

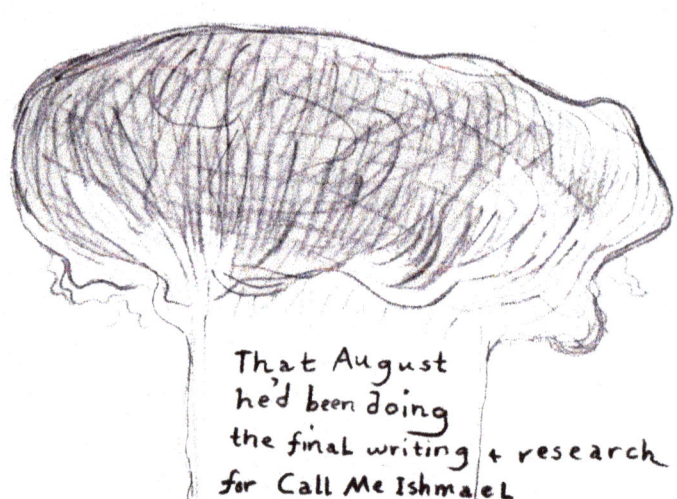

That August
he'd been doing
the final writing & research
for Call Me Ishmael

when General Groves
got his way
& Hiroshima & Nagasaki
were destroyed

Hiroshima was hit the day before
Olson visited the whaling museum in Nantucket
where he searched through old sailors' diaries
& found out for sure

in records of the ship Essex
which wrote of cannibalism
among some of the crew
after the Essex was hoved in by
a huge whale & sank
in Nov of 1820
leaving the crew adrift in open whaleboats.

The bombing of Hiroshima & Nagasaki
& sleuthing out the Essex diaries
solidified O's take
on the capable evil
"man devours man"

16

Visits to See Pound

—two periods of visiting
> Pound
separated by 8 months
when he was away from D.C.

first visit 1-4-46
> 24th visit, the final one,
>> on 2-24-48

Trip West in 1947

Met up with Kenneth Rexroth
> who introduced him to Muriel Rukeyser
>> Wm Everson, Mary Fabilli   \
> & urged by Rexroth
> met Robert Duncan

He met geographer Carl Sauer
> in the Earth Sciences Bldg of Berkeley
>> Sauer was working on Ice Ages

O worked in the
> Bancroft reading room
>> searching through Gold Rush materials

> and looking for Donner Party data
> plus studying the activities of John Sutter

A Black Mountain Summer
1948

> The summer at Black Mountain college
>> was organized by Josef Albers

> John Cage & Merce Cunningham were asked to come
> plus Buckminster Fuller and Willem de Kooning

> It was one of those summers
>> like The Summer of Love
>>> Monet's first waterlilies
>>> or the premiere of *Hamlet*

you might like to visit in a Time Machine

Its origins were rooted in the
        grove of olive trees near Athens
                where Plato taught
—the genius of cross-meshing out of doors
mind feeding mind
    art art
        and creativity creativity

in a tiny college living in a "constant state of crisis"
on the edge of the ever-moving palette knife of '48.

    De Kooning had sold nothing in his spring show
    Merce had left the Martha Graham company
        & had not yet formed his own

Robert Rauschenberg was on hand
        for the discipline of Albers.

The faculty was scraping by on rainbow stew
    & happy to get room & board
        and a beautiful *summer*
            in North Carolina.

Fuller at 52 was best known for his Dymaxion house & Dymaxion car
which had failed to get backing – someone was killed in an accident
& he had not been able to get mass production $ for the house

    He was experimenting with sleep patterns
    sleeping a half hour ever six hours
        apparently around the clock

Students worked hard
    to erect what *was* to be Fuller's first geodesic dome
        of venetian blind slats
            which turned out to be too thin.

Merce taught a class called Technique of Dancing
        & choreographed a few student dances
Someone built some Orgone Boxes

John Cage put on the
    Amateur Festival of the Music of Erik Satie
whose feature was a production of
Satie's "The Ruse of Medusa" on August 14
    translated from the French by M. C. Richards.
& a cast which included Fuller, Elaine & Willem de Kooning, Merce,
Cage, Arthur Penn

Beginning that fall
the bard from DC named Charles Olson
     began coming once a month to give lectures

The Wallace Campaign

There was massive red-baiting
of the Henry Wallace-Glen Taylor Progressive Party ticket
     by liberal democrats
     especially by a group called the
     Americans for Democratic Action

Communists were welcomed into the 1948
Henry Wallace coalition–

& Southerners who hated blacks
    formed the States' Rights Democrat party aka the Dixiecrats
    and ran Strom Thurmond of South Carolina for pres

"Keep America Human with Truman"
    was one of Harry's posters

In Woodstock, NY
historian Alf Evers
    worked to get out the vote for Wallace

Aug 5, '48
    Pete Seeger, who "Led the music at the Philadelphia
        Convention when Wallace was nominated"
    sang for 150 at Wallace rally in Woodstock

Klan Burns Crosses at Woodstock Wallace Rally

The local Klan burned fiery crosses & "hammers & sickles"
near Wallace rally in Woodstock

The Ulster County News for Sept 16 noted
    "Citizens Committee Presents Petition to Town Board on Cross Burnings"
    612 signatures on petitions for special meeting. Woodstock.
    ...Secretary of Woodstock Art Conference telegraphs Gov. Dewey
        to say 3 crosses have been burned in Woodstock
        within the past six months.

Kingston Daily Freeman June 17, 1948,

    250 at local rally for Wallace on June 16 at a local hotel

    Subjects: "control of monopolies and prices and taking the profits
        out of war were cited as the chief aims of the
            Wallace 'Peace Program.'"

Entertainment by the "Wallace Balladeers featured folk music and songs."

The Hostility Wallace Faced

An article in the Daily Freeman, August 31, 1948:

"Wallace Pelted with Eggs,"
stopped entirely from speaking in North Carolina
"Am I in America?" Wallace asked.

The Kingston Daily Freeman
August 31, 1948
announced that a cross was burned about 70 yards
from the Woodstock home of Howard Bird
president of the Woodstock Club for Wallace
while a meeting of Progressive Youth for Wallace
was being held

A resolution of the Woodstock Art Conference was sent to
Governor Dewey asking "immediate action"
at 10 o'clock as 100 young people
were assembled for a "Wallace rally."

Sept 11, "Swimming Hootenanny" for Wallace at J. Kingsbury's
place in Woodstock, with Pete Seeger as guest artist.
"Those attending were asked to bring guitars,
swim suits, blankets, and sweaters." They were urged to car pool:
"anyone have car space is asked to phone the Seegers."

Woodstock Henry Wallace Vote Nov. '48

	Dewey	Truman	Wallace
Dist 1	702	146	91
		Liberal 21	
Dist 2	397	26	19

Olson did what he could
for the national campaign

A Geodesic Dome at Black Mountain

Once in the '90s
on a visit to Black Mountain
our guide showed us what she said was
the spot where the first
        geodesic dome
constructed of slats
from Venetian blinds
      the summer of '49
(based on the model Fuller brought)
was built, then collapsed
into a pile
   o' slats

Fact or semi-fact?

Ed Sanders
2-8-18

Y & X was published in '49
and Frances Bolderoff
        responded with intense praise

A Manifesto:
Projective Verse
1950

O was working on a manifesto, *Projective Verse*
        and mailed the first draft of it early February
              to Frances Boldereff

She pleaded to come to O for a visit
        which he refused

"I love you so much I am full of music,"
        Frances Boldereff to O,
            sometime the first half of April

In a year of war, commie-noia & Joseph McCarthy giving
        Thomas Jefferson & the Constitution
                  a wave-off

William Carlos Williams wrote in late April to O
urging him to contact a poet in New Hampshire named
              Robert Creeley

    "Drop a note to Robert Creely (sic)
        in Littleton, N.H.

    —he's got some ideas and wants to USE them.
    Maybe you've already heard of him.

        Write.

    Send him anything you think is worth
        perpetuating."

& thus began a life-long friendship.

That late spring Olson sent Creeley
        a draft of "Projective Verse"
Creeley offered a few suggestions

June 5, '50 Cree' to O:
"form is never more than an *extension* of content"

July '50 re-write of Projective Verse

Creeley helped in the re-working
and later that year it was published in an issue of
    Poetry New York #3 1950

O's Manifesto was featured in WCW's
    "Autobiography" in '51

    & it commenced its
    world-wide Effect

one of the seed texts
    that pointed a path
        the next several generations of bards
                could explore

Projective Verse
Lightning Crackles

"ONE PERCEPTION MUST IMMEDIATELY AND DIRECTLY LEAD TO A FURTHER PERCEPTION"

and this:

"A poem is energy transferred from where the poet got it, by way of the poem itself to, all the way over to, the reader"

and:

"We now enter.... the large area of the whole poem, into the FIELD.... where all the syllables and all the lines must be managed in their relation to each other."

and this:

"Let me put it baldly. The two halves are:
    the HEAD, by way of the EAR, to the SYLLABLE
    the HEART, by way of the BREATH, to the LINE"

The First Maximus Poem
1950

Vincent Ferrini in Gloucester
wrote to O in D.C.
       on 5-3-50
asking for a poem for a magazine to be called
      Voyager

The O replied
with a letter to Ferrini
      the first Maximus poem

I, Maximus of Gloucester, to You

O who had campaigned for Henry Wallace
         in '44 & '48
kept his Wallacian Vision
in lines such as:

"5.
love is not easy
but how shall you know,
New England, now
that pejorocracy is here, how
that street-cars, o Oregon, twitter
in the afternoon, offend
a black-gold loin?

    how shall you strike,
o swordsman, the blue-red back
when, last night, your aim
was mu-sick, mu-sick, mu-sick
And not the cribbage game?

(o Gloucester-man,
weave
your birds and fingers
new, your roof-tops,
clean shit upon racks
sunned on
American
braid
with others like you, such
extricable surface
as faun and oral,
satyr lesbos vase

o kill kill kill kill
those
who advertise you
out....."

He took over the name of a 2nd century
      philosopher from Tyre
for his work as an Investigative Poet
  on current times as well as
      on the herodotean history
        of a 1623 fishing place
          named Gloucester

Our Lady of Good Voyage in the first Maximus

Across the street
from Destino's

where we always ate in Glou'

& I recall
Harvey Brown
        in 1987
                after dinner

kneeling on the steps of
        Our Lady of Good Voyage

opening the book
and reading the lines from the first Maximus:

"(o my lady of good voyage
        in whose arm, whose left arm rests
no boy but a carefully carved wood, a painted face, a schooner!
a delicate mast, as bow-sprit for

        forwarding"

Walking with Gerrit in Olson's Tansy Field

Gerrit cracked apart the
Tansy leaves—
 smelling like
walnut husks— he
 said he used them
in making omelets

 by the feather-mussy beach
 of Stage Fort Park

9-27-82

Tansy buttons, tansy
for my city
Tansy for their noses

Tansy for them,
tansy for Gloucester to take the smell
of all owners,
the smell

Tansy
for all of us

— from Letter 3

27

E.S.
2-12-18

A Journey to Sleuth Out Mayan Glyphs

On his fiscal own
Olson
    in December '50 learned
that he could withdraw several hundred dollars
        of retirement money
           from his work years prior
                for the Gloucester post office

Yay! He decided to withdraw it at once
& spend the cash on a trip to the Yucatán.

They'd learned of a beach house in Lerma
    rentable for $15 a month

        and planned their Voyage to Lerma
        subletting their apartment in D.C.
            then:

Mother Passes Away

Mother Mary passed away
two days before O's 40th.

Olson buried her in the Swedish cemetery in Worcester

disposed of her possessions
returned to D.C.
    and headed by bus to NOLA
then a Norwegian freighter
           to the Yucatán peninsula

then a bus down the coast to the tiny sea-side village Lerma
his and Connie's home for the next six months.

Actual Glyphs

He was on a bus heading south along
the Gulf coast of Yucatán

& saw out the window
a ruin with a steep pyramid

asks the driver to let him off

As Dennis Tedlock puts it in his remarkable
"The Olson Codex:

Projective Verse and the Problem
of Mayan Glyphs"

"He works his way through the rubble of the ruin
... He kneels to clear away from the face
of a partially buried stone
and finds what he has been hoping for:
glyphs"

"I hunt among stones"

1951

Ed Sanders 2-3-18

During the voyage Connie became pregnant.

O sent some 46 letters to Robert Creeley
using a typewriter he brought with him

He was on a bus heading south along
the Gulf coast of Yucatán

& saw out the window
a ruin with a steep pyramid

 asks the driver to let him off

 As Dennis Tedlock puts it in his remarkable book
 The Olson Codex: Projective Verse and the Problem
    of Mayan Glyphs

 "He works his way through the rubble of the ruin....
 He kneels to clear away from the face
   of a partially buried stone
    and finds what he has been hoping for: glyphs."

   Leaving Yucatán

 "I was very happy in Yucatán,"
    he said later
 Didn't want to leave
 He would "have loved to continue...."

 He and Connie took a lumber boat to Pensacola
 on July 6. About to leave, O to Cree':
 "God, but we shall miss
    what we have wrought
       here."
 Then off to Black Mountain.

Black Mountain Glyph Exchange
Summer '51

O brought the Spirit of the Glyph
to Black Mountain college
    where they had a "Glyph Exchange" that summer
among the guest faculty.
Ben Shahn traded Charles Olson
    a drawing *A Glyph for Charles* for a poem
        called "Glyph"
& then Katherine Litz created a dance called *Glyph*
with a set by Shahn, music by Lou Harrison
    & words by Mr. O

All hail the Glyph

Human Universe

While still in the Yucatan
he was writing this essay-manifesto

sending the first draft on June 17 to both
Cid Corman & to Cree'

after that editing & re-working
till Sept. 15 it was off
    for the Winter '51-'52
        issue of *Origen*

(When I organized the New Amazing Grace verses
in the early '90s, gathering over 100
from poets, musicians & writers:
    Anselm Hollo's saluted Olson:

    "I praise each day dawns on our bed
    to light your human form
    here next to mine when night has fled
    and we are here once more

    together in this raging world
    this human universe
    together in this human world
    this raging universe")

  In "Human Universe," Olson's belief
  that "Form is nothing more than an extent of content"
  led him to strongly criticize the idealism, say, of Plato:

whose "world of Ideas," O wrote,
    "of forms as extricable from content,
    is as much and as dangerous an issue
       as are logic and classification,
and they need to be seen as such if we are to get on
to some alternative to the whole Greek system.

"Plato may be a honey head, as Melville called him,
but he is precisely that—
    treacherous to all ants...."

  He was astounded by the hieroglyphs
  how the Maya "were able to stay so interested
  in the expression and gestures of all creatures, including
  at least three planets in addition to the human face,
  eyes and hands, that they invented a system of
    written record, now called hieroglyphs,
    which, on its very face, is verse,
    the signs were so clearly and densely chosen
    that, cut in stone, they retain the power of
  the objects of which they are the images...."

    —Living Glyphs
    like the Egyptians
    who thought their Glyphs
        were alive.

O First Positing "Postmodern"

Olson coined the term Postmodern
in a letter to Creeley from Black Mountain
                              ca October 20, 1951

In the text of this long long letter
                        is the following:

"(I am even worked to the persuasion that one of the reasons
why we have such few records of the so-called past, or
prehistory, is, not that man was not 'advanced' but that by the
very conditions above described as previous state to discourse,
there was no reason why man needed to *record*: he acted,
instead. And this was his glory, this was what made him
more man than he has been. Simply, there was too much *life*
to be wasting it, in texts!

       "In other words, what we do have is enough:: look at rock
paintings, and all the clay, the worked or written-on clay!
Look at the Venus of Mentone!

                                      "What else do we want?   And
had we not, ourselves (I mean post-modern man), better just
leave such things behind us— and not so much trash of
discourse, & gods?"

But, what does O mean by "post-modern"?

It certainly doesn't mean "the salivating dogs of Eternity
                                         always push onward"

or no matter how "modern"
              and exuberantly "Out There in Orbit"

       we are

       we tend to make ourselves
       obsolete...

        Postmodern?
        Well, for sure things
        after Pound, Williams, Eliot,
        Thomas, Good Fences Make Good Neighbors,
        et al. became a bit postmarked

Postmodern is not that,
rather he seems to be
talking about a poetics that
searches the glyphs & vestiges of the past

        He was pointing his finger
        toward a New Archaic
                        (I think)

        Discussing in his long letter to Creeley
        "a way to define THE ARCHAIC
        as the condition for which
                we can be thankful as our
                present one."

and this: that
"there is no end to awe"…..

after the "classical" age
of Platonic discourse
        & the rattle of the gods
an Age of a New Archaic

Fragmented stories of the deeds
of men & women
                especially in the past & present
                of Gloucester

allowing for a
        "park of
                eternal events."

Kate was Born

At the Asheville Hospital
    on 10-23-51
    Connie gave birth to

    Katherine Mary (Olson)
    the 1st names of their parents' moms

The O pad
in South Lodge

was adorned w/ streamers o' tinfoil

Olson soon wrote "An Ode to Nativity"

"Letter for Melville 1951"

fiercely announcing that he was the guardian of Melville scholarship

a verse argument composed after an invitation
    to a conference of the Melville Society
    celebrating the 100th anniversary
        of *Moby-Dick*

    held at Williams College

The "Melville Letter" was published
as a pamphlet by the Black Mountain press.

The Brain Police Visit the Bard

    Two times that year (1952)
    the Brain Police & the Belief Fuzz
    i.e., the FBI
    visited Black Mountain College
        to ask Olson
        about the Office of War Information
        from which he had resigned
            because of political interference

The FBI also wanted to know
        about O's lobbying work at the United Nations

He wrote to Creeley
        about the Not-so-Secret Inquisitor visit:

"My life (my fate) is herewith interfered with
....I have to feel that shadow — this must be the
        old European thing anew,
            the SECRET police"

1953

Spg of '53 Jonathan Williams asked for a book
so April O wrote six new Maximuses
            adding to the 4 already done

Maximus Poems 1-10
published fall '53

    by Williams' Jargon Press

& dedicated

        "for ROBERT CREELEY
        —the Figure of Outward"

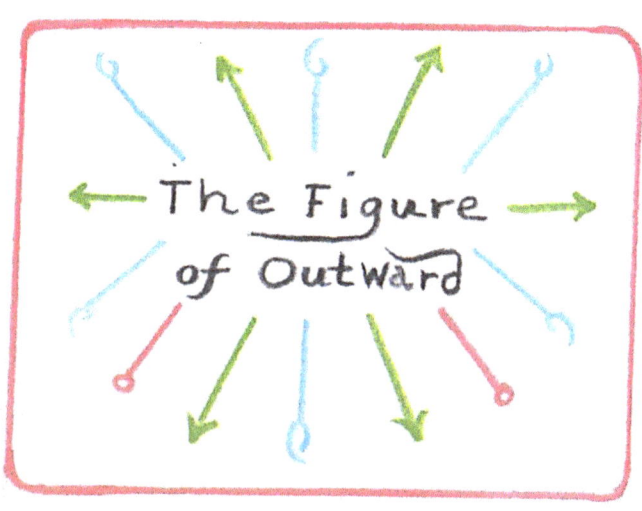

Poeta: et Historicus

In October of '53
Olson sent a final addendum
 to Mayan Letters
to Creeley in Mallorca, ending:

"The trouble is,
 it is very difficult,
 to be both a poet
 an anhistorian."

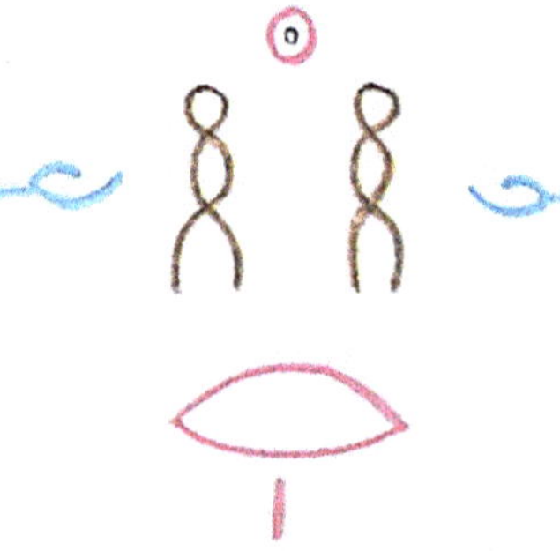

1953 O Praising John Smith in his review of a book about Smith (later printed in Human Universe & Other Essays

and as I traced in
"America, a History in Verse, The 17th century":

"My bardic mentor Charles Olson
was much impressed with the work of John Smith
He wrote an essay on the book Captain John Smith, His Life & Legend,
by Bradford Smith (Lippincott 1953)

wherein Olson praises Smith's "own exceeding fine nine books.....published
1608 to 1631."

O: "The wild thing about the original Smith is this business, that
it may damn well have been the very bite in his language, which
did break his life in half, did make him the failure he took himself,
did keep him from ever getting backing again, to get back to the
States [to Virginia]— kept him exiled in London, the first one who wanted
out, the man who, by 1614, knew the country as not only not one other did
(not even a West Country fisherman) but said it in prose like
as no one has since, simply that he had the first of it, had it not like
even Columbus did, but as Columbus' navigator say, only Smith
said it, got it into words, didn't as Juan de la Cosa did so
handsomely, by a map [in 1500]."

That Smith, as a good writer,
provided the Primal Take
on the new wilderness
that became the U.S.A.

Smith sent the Virginia Company "a map.... The whole middle
coast. So known, so done, the states still stand their
boundaries by it. The sort of knowledge Smith gave
Hudson, in another letter, Hudson went straight to
the river. How Smith later knew New England,
named her that, put her down in prose I can feel
now the way his boat bent along the same coasts I know—
mind you, he was doing it for one of the very first times,
it's a different thing, to feel a coast, an ancient thing
this Smith had, what men had to have before Pytheas, to move...."

—Olson

Knowing the New Facts Early

"Smith was one man who knew the new facts early."

—Charles Olson, in his essay on Smith"

Olson was a
praiser of
    Captain John Smith

as "the psyche that split off
and went to America
at exactly that
      moment of
Shakespeare, Daniel,
   & Campion"

  as George Butterick noted
in his 12-1-64 class notes
      attending O's courses
         at Buffalo

Dancing while strapped into a Rocking Chair

how to dance sitting down

—Maximus I.35

(or Samuel Beckett in "Murphy")

Rock-Dancing

The Maximus Poem is titled
>Tyrian Businesses

written in the spring of '53
with section two,
>an inspiration to some of us over the years
>as follows:

>"how to dance
>sitting down"

Olson had first seen Martha Graham perform
in D.C. n '39

had sent her his dance-play based on
>Moby-Dick, "The Fiery Hunt"

He may have been referring to Graham
but I like also Beckett's "Murphy"
>who tied himself up in a rocking chair
>& rock-danced

*how to dance
sitting down*
—Maximus I.35

The Reasons for the Present

Spring 1954

He held a class on "the reasons, causes and consequences of the present"

He had the Ashville Citizen-Times
    dropped off near the
        college entrance
                each morning
So he and students
could discuss the meanings behind the meanings
        of current news.

The Army-McCarthy hearings were broadcast
by the U.S. Senate
        April-June,
Olson and students watched the
hearings on the only TV available—
    in the house of the man who ran
            the Black Mountain farm.
    They probably watched Joseph Welch's
    famous rebuke of Senator McCarthy:

"You have done enough. Have you no sense of decency?"

As Ἡροδότου of Halicarnassos

I would be an historian as Herodotus was, looking for himself for the evidence of what is said...

Maximus I
Letter 23

Dorcester fishermen (just arrived) took over a Pilgrim-built fishing stage
 in Gloucester 1623-24
& plymouth-men (Myles Standish) came to fight over it
 the next year

Olson describes it:

> What we have in this field in these scraps among these fishermen, and the Plymouth men, is more than the fight of one colony with another, it is the whole engagement against (1) mercantilism (cf. the Westcountry men and Sir Edward Coke against the Crown, in Commons, these same years—against Gorges); and (2) against nascent capitalism except as it stays the individual adventurer and the worker on share—against all sliding statism, ownership getting in to, the community as, Chambers of Commerce, or theocracy; or City Manager

E.S.
2-12-1?

Betty Kaiser

Betty Kaiser (as Solveig) & O (plus others) acted in a Black Mntn production of Peer Gynt & Betty performed Stepan Wolpe's setting of "Solveig's Song"

— It was Love.

Then in Sept she was pregnant & went to stay w/ her sister Jean Radoslovich in N. Brunswick, NJ where she decided to have the child with O

1954

Meeting John Wieners
October 1954

On the day Hurricane Hazel struck
O read at the Charles St. Meeting House

gave out copies of the *Black Mntn Review*

including to 20-year old John Wieners
then after graduating from Boston College in 1954,

he enrolled in the last class of Black Mountain College

Deciding to Live with Betty
Early February '56

A sad sad final discussion with Connie
in which Olson announced his intention
                              to live with Betty

Connie was weeping
"I don't want you to go. I don't want you to go."

"I must go," said Charles several times

then drove away in his heat-less Ford

(so wrote Connie's sister, Jane Atherton)

March 1956
       Olson arrived at Black Mountain
                      with Betty and Charles Peter

That fall Jonathan Williams published
                    Maximus Poems / 11-22

Black Mountain Closes

O remained there with Betty and Charles Peter
 getting it ready to sell

January 1957
 O writes "The Librarian"

Lectures in San Francisco
February 1957

O, Betty and baby Charles Peter by train to S.F.
where he delivered "The Special View of History" lectures
 in San Francisco
  then returned to the complications
   of closing down Black Mountain

The Question of Polis

In Henry Ferrini's film *Polis is This*
Amiri Baraka said,

> "To me, Olson's concept of the polis was just simply
> the idea that you had to be grounded in the concerns
> of the people, that the people are finally
> the makers of history, and that you have to be
> grounded in what is historical in that sense.
> What are the concerns of the people?"

HISTORY IS THE NEW LOCALISM

February '57

O's Five Day Lecture Cycle the "Special View of History"

"History is the new localism, a polis to replace the one which was lost in various stages all over the world from 490 B.C. on, until anyone of us knows places where it is disappearing right now."

— The Special View of History

&

From my 1983 Olson Memorial Lectures:

Maximus

He will be Gloucester

Encompassing it,

Nut above it, Geb Below

πόλις

...Gloucester,
where Polis
still thrives

    Letter 5
    1.22

polis is
eyes

    Letter 6
    1.26

So few
have the polis
in their eye

    Letter 6
    1.28

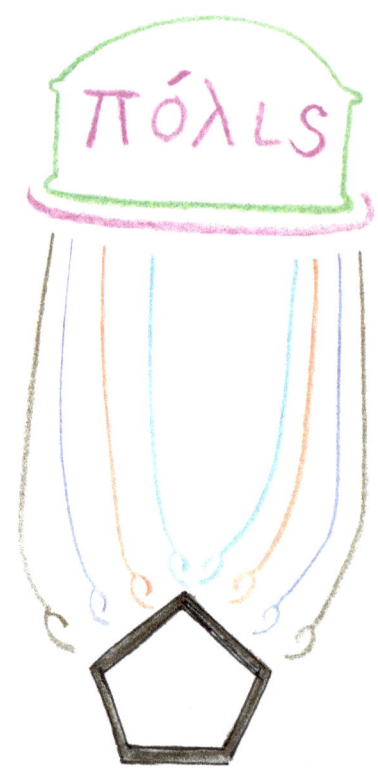

Can the Polis of Charles Olson transform the ⬠ into peace-make?

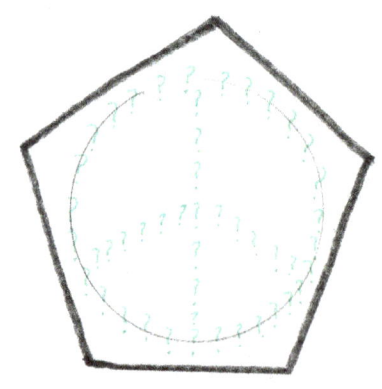

polis
is this
πόλις αὔτη ἔστιν

    An American
is a complex of occasions,
themselves a geometry
of spatial nature.

    I have this sense,
that I am one
with my skin

    Plus this — plus this:
that forever the geography
which leans in
on me I compell
backwards I compell Gloucester
to yield, to
change
    Polis
is this

—from
Maximus to Gloucester,
Letter 27 [withheld]
II.15

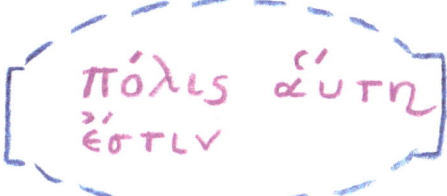

E.S.
2-28-18

Placing His Dreams

Καὶ γάρ τ' ὄναρ ἐκ Διός ἐστιν

A dream is from Zeus
—Homer
Book 1, The Iliad L. 63

Odysseus spoke with the ghost
        of his mother Anticlea
She told him she had passed away
        from longing for her son's return
Three times he reached out
        to hold his sweet mother's phantom
and three times she flew through his arms
        like a shadow or a dream
—Odyssey Book 11

In his 1956 poem, "As the Dead Prey Upon Us"
He finds his mother, in a dream,
sitting in a rocker in the house to which she returns
once a week. There's a blue deer also in the dream
& other entities, & he exclaims:

    "o peace, mother, for the mammothness
      of the comings and goings
      of the ladders of life"

E.S.
2-18-18

The Librarian

A Dream Poem in January 1957

...Where is Bristow? When does I-A get me home? I am caught

in Gloucester. (What's buried behind Lufkin's Diner? Who is

Frank Moore?

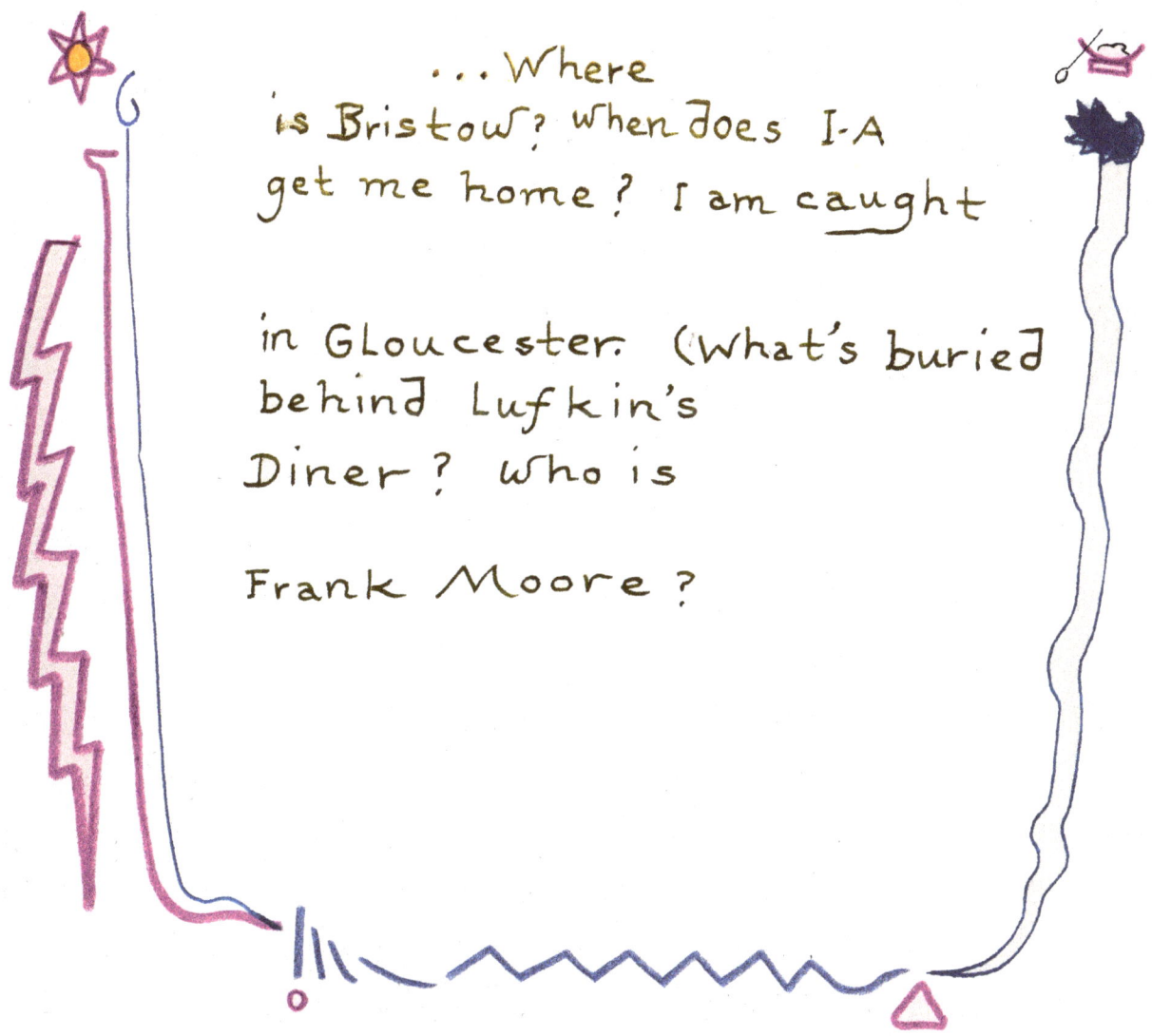

καὶ γάρ τ' ὄναρ ἐκ Διός ἐστιν

A dream is from Zeus
 Book 1, The Iliad

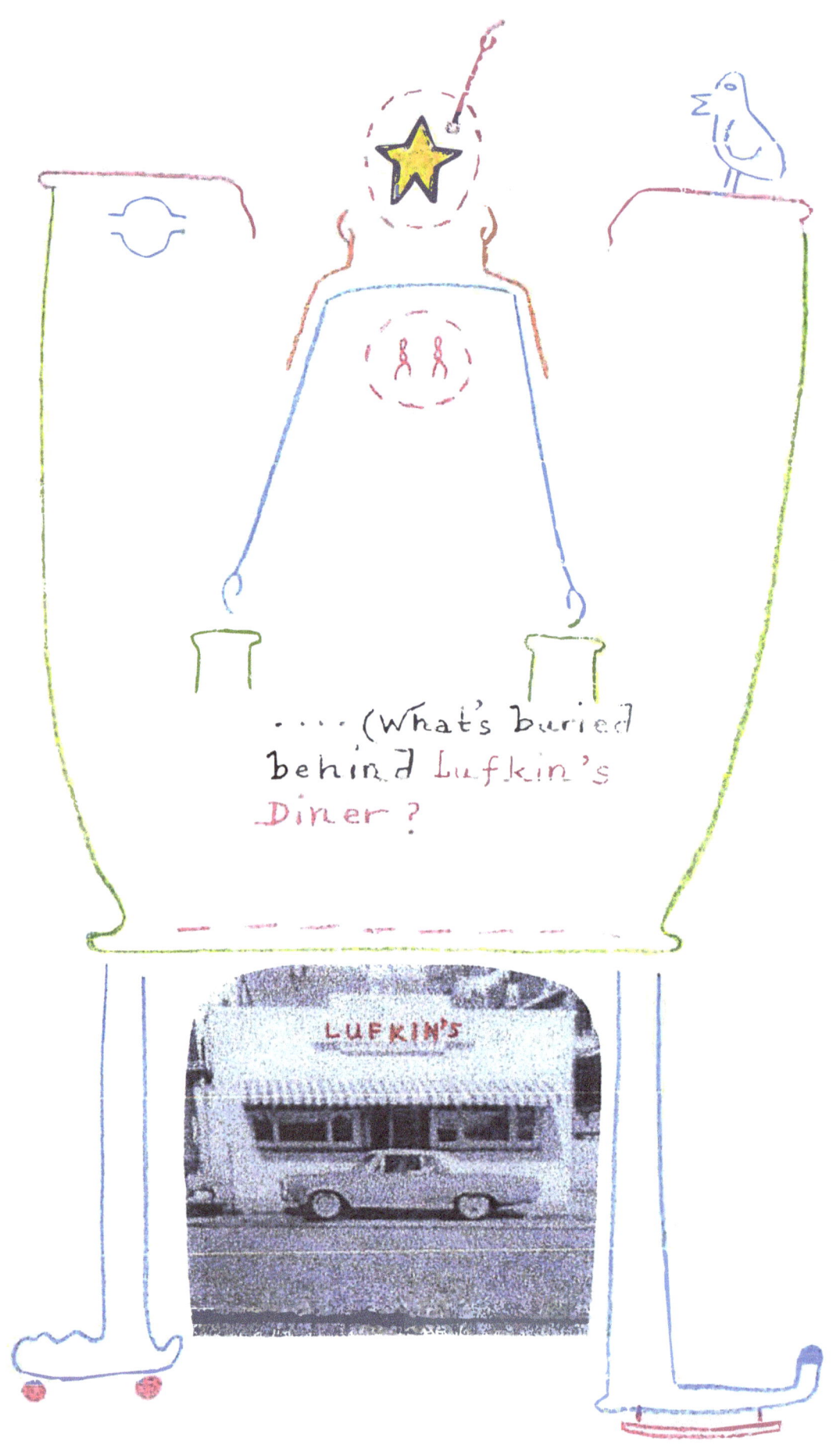

1957

54

Moving to Gloucester
August 1957

Olson, as Rector,
closed Black Mountain College
for dearth of funds
& Betty looked for a place to live
      in Gloucester

In a letter of July 25, 1957
Betty wrote an excited letter:

"Have just found a wonderful
   crazy apartment. The
   rooftops of Gloucester.
   No stove, no refrigerator, no heat—
   but light, o Charles, the light!

"And a little balcony
    to look at the ocean, & gulls
    flocks of gulls,

"Right at the wharf, 28 Fort Square,
Do you know it?
And now to Garbo, and Grand Hotel.

"I wish you were with me—
your body— my darling man—
I miss your body

   Betty"

Shortly after the letter
the couple
   and young Charles Peter

moved into the apartment at 28 Fort Square
      in Gloucester

   (which he kept all the way to his finality
    in early 1970)

Door & Porch
of the bard

1957-1969

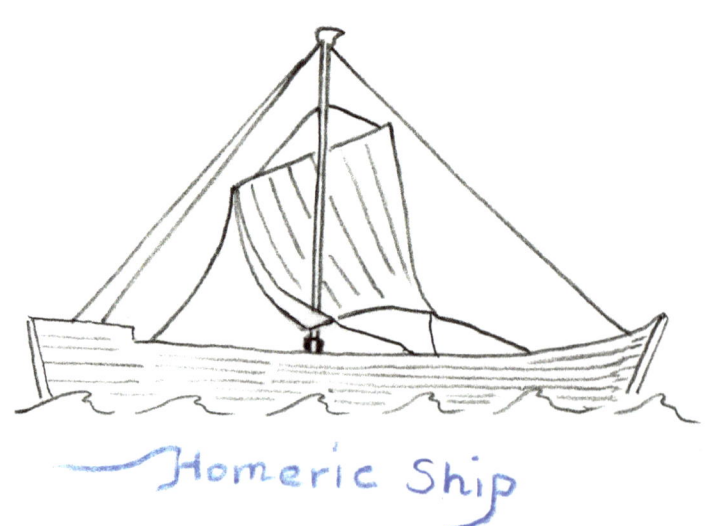
Homeric Ship

Topos, Typos, Tropos

These three words
surfaced in Olson's
1959 letter to
    Elaine Feinstein:

"The basic trio wld seem to be:
topos/typos/tropos, 3 in 1."

9 years later, in the Beloit Lectures,
he said:

'I can't get away from any of them'
       p. 42 *Poetry & Truth*

"Topos... it means simply place.
But again place has too much
familiarity in America." p. 42

O in the same lecture said that
"tonight my job is to see if
I can characterize what, in using
the word type or typos
I mean by the blow upon
the world." p. 54

Tropos

ὁ trópos
a turn, direction, way, habit
custom, character

Tropé
ἡ τροπή
turning around, change

> the Blow is Creation
> & the Twist   the Nasturtium
> is any one of Ourselves
> And the Place of it all
>   Mother   Earth   Alone
>
>   Maximus III 226

Edward Sanders
4-28-18

1959 for O

In March, O began the poems for
                             Maximus II

O met Allen Ginsberg and Gregory Corso
                at a much anticipated reading in Boston
                                        (or Harvard)

               When I first met Ginsberg in 1964
               he told me he put a sign "writing"
               on the front door of his pad
                     (no one had phones back then)
                     to ask to be allowed to write sans disturbance

               And later I learned
               the O had a "Do Not Disturb" sign
               for the kitchen door at 28 Fort Square.

May '59 Totem Press published O's letter in response
               to a letter to him from poet Elaine Feinstein

On November 20 Don Allen visited Olson
        with Phil Whalen, LeRoi Jones, Michael McClure
        & David Cummings

O took them on a tour of Dogtown
the rocky terminal glacial moraine on Gloucester's edge
        with ruins of cellars and old old houses
        and during the visit, McClure noted
        women in the distance
               picking low-lying evergreen boughs
                            for holiday decor

In Dogtown he told them the story of Andrew Merry
a sailer who lived, as O wrote,
               "by Jeremiah Millet's house"

& who successfully wrestled an ever-growing young bull
but it had become dangerous
               so Merry ceased

   but then invited all his acquaintances
   to watch him wrestle the bull
        for a final time
        on a Sunday in 1892

Olson pointed out the exact location of the bull's enclosure

   But then after drinking aplenty on the Saturday night
   before the Sunday encounter
   Andrew Merry went out to take on
        the bull
   and he was gored to death

After Allen and the others left Gloucester that evening
Olson wrote "Maximus from Dogtown— I

The Distances 1960

The Maximus Poems 1960

   In 1961 I purchased *The Maximus Poems*
   & the Auerhahn Press publication of "Maximus from Dogtown— I"
   in the Eighth Street Bookshop
       near Washington Square Park
       and New York University

   & was, in the parlance of the era, was "blown away" especially at first
       by the poem with the references to Hesiod's *Theogony*
       the Andrew Merry's battle
         with the bull of Dogtown

The Dogtown Writing Tree

Olson
writing on
a make-shift
writing desk
nailed to a tree
in Dogtown

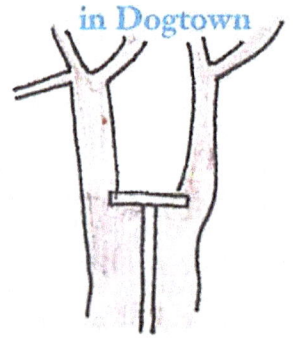

Near Gravel Hill
by the entrance
      to Dogtown
off Cherry Street

where Olson led his visitors
    (including Don Allen, Michael McClure, &
        David Cummings)

in Nov '59

to show them
    the chest-high board
    nailed to a tree
    & supported by a cross-beam & post

& how he would stand at the writing-tree
and, on this occasion,
    demonstrating with a tree branch
        to serve as a pen

(See *Maximus II.37*)

1959

Maximus from Dogtown - I

The sea was born of the earth without sweet union of love Hesiod says

But that then she lay for heaven and she bare the thing which encloses every thing, Okeanos the one which all things are and by which nothing is anything but itself, measured so

screwing earth, in whom love lies which unnerves the limbs and by its heat floods the mind and all gods and men into further nature

Vast earth rejoices

ἡ δὲ καὶ ἀτρύγετον πέλαγος τέκεν, οἴδματι θυῖον
Πόντον, ἄτερ φιλότητος ἐφιμέρου· αὐτὰρ ἔπειτα
Οὐρανῷ εὐνηθεῖσα τέκ' Ὠκεανὸν βαθυδίνην

Earth bore the barren sea, Pontos,
without any sweetness of love
& then she lay with Heaven
& bore him deep-swirling Okeanos

Theogony ll. 131-133

Ὣς φάτο· γήθησεν δὲ μέγα φρεσὶ Γαῖα πελώρη

Thus he spoke
 & vast earth
  rejoiced
   in her great heart

Theogony l. 173

61

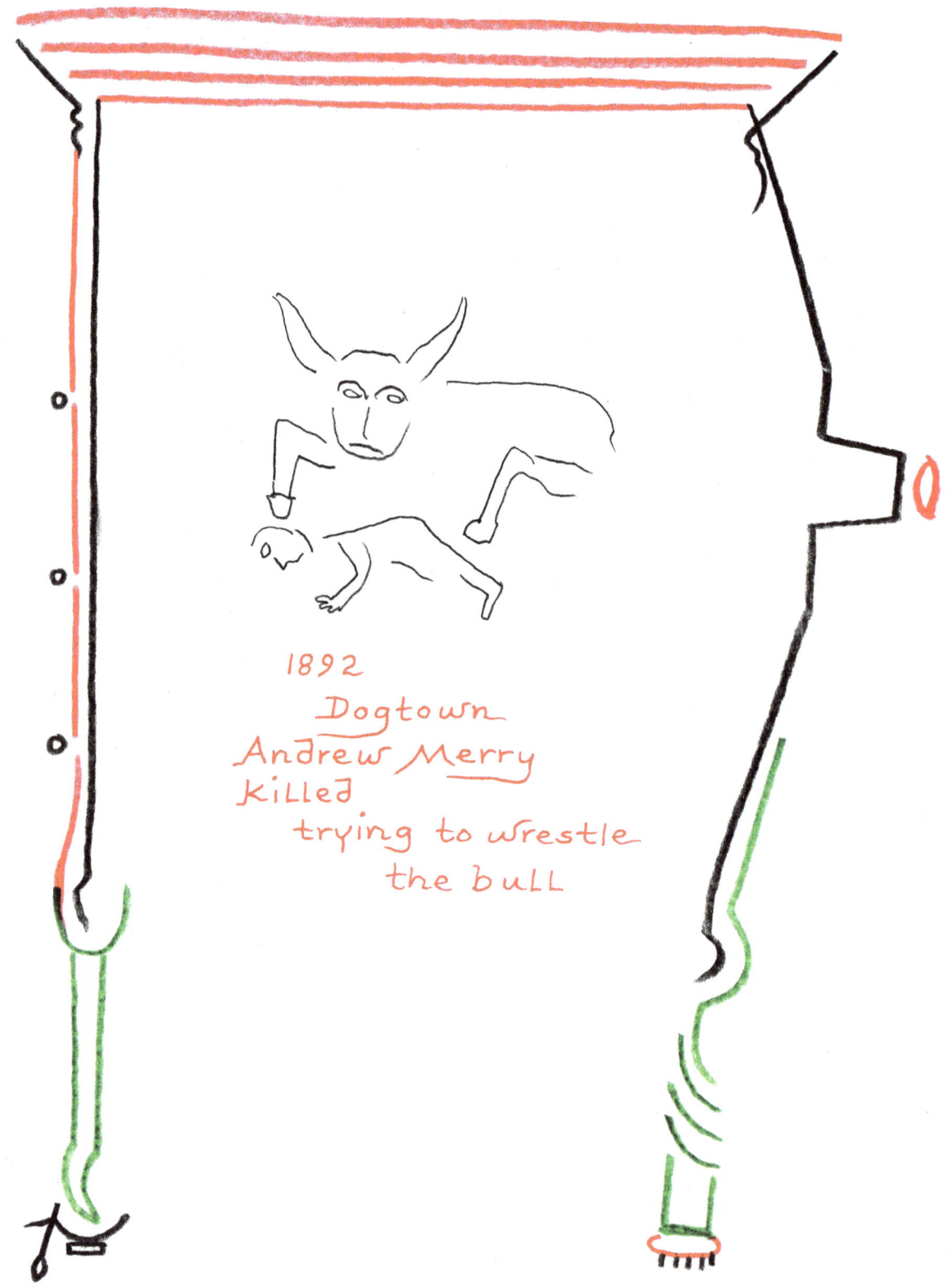

Betty Kaiser Olson
He was very erotically attracted to her
& she to him.

Like other men
with pretty wives
or mates
O was a bit worried
about others
hitting on her

*A Performance of
Maximus from Dogtown—I
Wheeler Auditorium
Berkeley — February 23, 1991*

This is a story poem
written on 11-20-1959
after a visit to Dogtown
        in Gloucester
with Michael MClure, Don Allen &
LeRoi Jones

(Phil Whalen was also on hand, but under the weather
so stayed on the couch in O's apartment at 28 Fort Square.)

It was printed in 1961
by Auerhahn Press in San Francisco
in a beautiful edition w/
an inspiring introduction
        by McClure.

It was one of the poems
that changed my life
It showed to me that a
poet can safely & without duplicity
make myth.
This story poem— Maximus from Dogtown— 1
tells the story of James Merry, a 6' 7" sailor,
who was known to wrestle & defeat
a growing bull calf in Dogtown.
He was due to wrestle the bull
one Sunday— The Saturay before
he was out drinking
The men in the tavern may
have taunted him— so
he went out about
midnight to test the bull
and Merry was gored to death.
In this poem Olson uses
portions of the creation myths

in Hesiod's *Theogony* — how the
sea was born from the
earth without an act of love—
but that then Earth or Gaia commingled w/
heaven, the sky, and deep-swirling Okeanos,
the watery abyss "above & below" &
around everything, was born.

There are also Egytian elements
to the poem— The Sky Goddess Nut,
for instance, & her consort, the
earth god, Geb.

It's vey much a poem
of our time— a time of war—
it's a poem of macho, of taunting,
of Gaia & heaven— of contest,
violence, excess, egomania
& the triumph
of that process known as Gaia

        In addition, of course, to Charles
        Olson, I would like
        to dedicate
        the recitation of
        this poem
                to the memory of
                      Harvey Brown.
        Ed Sanders
        Berkeley A.M.
        2-23-91

Magic Mushrooms

At Tim Leary's place on Nov. 26, 1960
Allen Ginsberg
took some psilocybin
      and had a Vast Experience
      among which he believed
      he could cure
      Leary's poor hearing
      & repair his weak eyes

        Leary was hesitant
        to allow the naked Ginsberg
        roam the streets of Cambridge
        to preach love
        zonked by the Mageia 'Shrooms

Allen took seriously his
psychedelic experiences with Tim Leary

to the point where he felt he had to proselytize
                                          their use

Among the first he turned on to psilocybin
were Thelonious Monk, Dizzy Gillespie, Franz Kline,
Willem de Kooning, and Robert Lowell

        That December Ginzap
        coaxed O
        to try psilocybin

a mushroom derivative
in pink-hued small-pill form

O drove to Cambridge
to see researchers at
the Harvard Psychology Dept
      Frank Baron & Tim Leary
& was brought to the "Mushroom House"
in Newton

As O recounted it later:
"when I took it I
was so high on bourbon
that I took it like
    it was a bunch of peanuts.

I kept throwing the
peanuts, and the mushroom,
    into my mouth"

Olson Experiences Being in a Native Longhouse on Psilocybin

"For example, the first time I went under the mushroom
I went into a big all longhouse take. I discovered a great
truth of the Indians of the territory, who discovered the
Longhouse Principle late, as you know. But we don't know
too much in anthropology yet about the history
    of the Longhouse
before the Dekanawidah epic. The epic may have
itself been the result of an Indian experience which hadn't
solidified itself before the Longhouse....

"I'm saying that the [psilocybin house] in Newton
in the mushroom house under the drug for me
was a longhouse, and I so said, 'My god,' I said,
'here we are. This is longhouse. Let's... oh wonderful,'

like, and we started to improvise."

    (The Gratwick Tape, November 16, 1963)

Olson's First Trip on Psilocybin

As O recounted later
"when I took it
I was so high on bourbon
that I took it
like it was a bunch of
    peanuts —
I kept throwing the
   peanuts, and the
mushrooms
       into my mouth"

—December 1960

An Archaeologist of Morning

"This is the morning, after the dispersion, and the work of the morning is methodology: how to use oneself, and on what. That is my profession.
I am an archaeologist of morning."

— The Present is Prologue

from 1952 but true through his life

Fame Amidst the Mallet of Pov
1960-1962

O's fame, in spite of the Mallet of Pov,
was rising because, among other things,
of the success of Don Allen's
       New American Poetry
which began with "The Kingfishers"
    & 40 pp of O's poetry

    & then at the Anthology's close
       "Projective Verse"

  going through 20 printings
        & spreading
       the O word worldwide.

To ward off the Mallet
    he began doing reading gigs
    so common to poets

    such as the Wesleyan Spring Poetry Festival
    in April o' '60

Later that year helped by cash gifts
      from an un-mentioned sponsor

In May '61 Cree' visited Olson
    while on a reading tour

    & discovered O had only $1 on hand
    He suggested O selling his archive
    so O offered the original annotated typescript
      of "Projective Verse" to Indiana U
        which offered such a small amount for it
          that he decided to hold on to it

February 14, 1962 O read at Harvard
    and soon thereafter a small tour through upper New England—
      Dartmouth, and Goddard College

Ed Dorn visiting him in July '62
found O utterly whacked by the Mallet of Pov
with Betty fishing off the pier for food
& the refrigerator un-working
      & resting in the back yard

O told Dorn
    he might relieve the Mallet
    by working at a fish processing plant.

Olson Singing The Truth of Pov

Song 3

    This morning of the small snow
I count the blessings, the leak in the faucet
which makes of the sink time, the drop
of the water on water as sweet
as the Seth Thomas
in the old kitchen
my father stood in his drawers to wind (always
he forgot the 30th day, as I don't want to remember
the rent
       a house these days
so much somebody else's
especially
Congoleum's

        Or the plumbing
that it doesn't work, this I like, have even used paper clips
as well as string to hold the ball up   And flush it
with my hand
     But that the car doesn't,
          that no moving thing moves
without that song I'd void my car of, the musickracker
of all ownership...
        Holes
in my shoes, that's all right, my fly
gaping, me out
at the elbows, the blessing
          that difficulties are once more

"In the midst of plenty, walk
  as close to
bare
     In the face of sweetness,
piss
       In the time of goodness,
go side, go
smashing, beat them, go as
(as near as you can

tear

In the land of plenty, have
nothing to do with it
       take the way of
the lowest,
including
your legs, go
contrary, go

sing

The Mallet of Pov
for Olson, Blake & others

"succession of employment." O! that I could live as others do in a regular

William Blake in 1803

(that leaves
  plenty of time
     to read & to write)

HE WHO WALKS WITH HIS HOUSE ON HIS HEAD

> he who walks with his house on
> his head is heaven he
> who walks with his house
> on his head is heaven he who walks
> with his house on his head
> —Maximus II   141

The O, utilizing a book titled
Algonquin Legends of New England
traces how a man traversing the woods
came across another man "carrying his house
on his head."

He-who-carried-his-house-on-his-Head
traded the House for a tanned raccoon skin the 1st guy
had with him

And the second man then donned the head-house
and he found it as "light as a basket"

So he ventured forth with his new house
He set it down at night
and slept in it very well
& there was plenty of food hanging
from the ceiling beams

and, as Olson points out, when the man
reached out for the dangling food
"the rug itself melted
and it was white snow, and his arms turned into wings
and he flew up to the food and it was birch-boughs on
which it hung,
   and he was a partridge and it was spring."

Chanted:
> he who walks with his house on
> his head is heaven he
> who walks with his house
> on his head is heaven he who walks
> with his house on his head

he who walks with his house on his head is heaven he who walks with his house on his head is heaven he who walks with his house on his head

Maximus II 141

A Difficult Poet

Χάος

Nulla dies sine linea

Mallet of Pov

"O that I could live as others do in a regular succession of employment"
—William Blake in 1803

"Ἔρος λυσιμελής
(Limber-Wanded Eros)

ultraretentive Memory

Mother of the Μουσάων Ἑλικωνιάδων

CAREER

(that leaves plenty of time to read & to write and to avoid the Fame Trap)

Cistern of the MUSES

Outward Projective Make it New

Hurler of O-Bolts

24/7

75

Edward Sanders
3-21-18

From Blake's Jerusalem

Los: Poetry, power of creative imagination

Beulah: Subconscious

Orb: place of dreams, poetry & inspiration

Jerusalem

Chap. 3.

But Los, who is the Vehicular Form of strong Urthona
Wept vehemently over Albion where Thames currents spring
From the rivers of Beulah; pleasant river! soft, mild, parent stream
And the roots of Albions Tree enterd the Soul of Los
As he sat before his Furnaces clothed in sackcloth of hair
In gnawing pain dividing him from his Emanation;
Inclosing all the Children of Los time after time.
Their Giant forms condensing into Nations & Peoples & Tongues
Translucent the Furnaces, of Beryll & Emerald immortal:
And Seven-fold each within other: incomprehensible
To the Vegetated Mortal Eye's perverted & single vision
The Bellows are the Animals Lungs. the hammers, the Animal Heart
The Furnaces, the Stomach for Digestion; terrible their fury
Like seven burning heavens rang'd from South to North

Here on the banks of the Thames. Los builded Golgonooza.
Outside of the Gates of the Human Heart, beneath Beulah
In the midst of the rocks of the Altars of Albion. In fears
He builded it. in rage & in fury. It is the Spiritual Fourfold
London: continually building & continually decaying desolate!
In eternal labours: loud the Furnaces & loud the Anvils
Of Death thunder incessant around the flaming Couches of
The Twentyfour Friends of Albion and round the awful Four
For the protection of the Twelve Emanations of Albions Sons
The Mystic Union of the Emanation in the Lord; Because
Man divided from his Emanation is a dark Spectre
His Emanation is an ever-weeping melancholy Shadow
But she is made receptive of Generation thro' mercy
In the Potters Furnace, among the Funeral Urns of Beulah
From Surrey hills, thro' Italy and Greece. to Hinnoms vale.

Urthona, the Northern Zoa; a blacksmith, constantly making forms

Albion / England

Emanation "is the feminine portion, or 'counterpart,' of the fundamentall bisexual mate" p 120

Los's polis of "Art & Manufacture"

at the total end Los is "reabsorbed" into Urthona

"Above Albion's 12 sons are Jerusalems sons & all the 12 Tribes spreading over Albion."

Hinnom Valley where children were sacrificed to Moloch (see Jeremiah vii:31)

Think Olson is Difficult?

O cistern
of the
Μοῦσαι

Assist me
as I sleuth

The Past

A Hant or Haint on Fort Hill

from spring of 1963

Maximus, to Gloucester, Letter 157

           an old Indian chief as hant
           sat on the rock between
           Tarantino's and Mr
           Randazza so he ran back into
           his house

The house I live in, and exactly on the back stairs,
is the sight

of the story
told me by

Mr Misuraca, that,
his mother, reports

that, the whole Fort Section, is
a breeding ground of the ghosts of,

dogs, and that, on those very steps, she saw,
as a girl, a fierce, blue, dog, come at her

as she was going out, the door.....

Thomas & Antonio Randazza fishermen, were neighbors of Olson on Fort Square — in O's words, on Randazza's side of Fort Hill

an Indian chief is buried there & there the Indian chief was sitting, 1959, on the stone Mr Randazza went white & went into his house

Always Researching & sleuthing

Said Mrs Tarantino,
occupying the yellow house
on fort constructed like
a blockhouse house said

You have a long nose, meaning
You stick it into every other person's
business, do you not? And I couldn't
say anything
but that I
do.

        Olson
          Maximus III 10

1963

Letters & Magazines to O
& Poems from Him to Publish

I started corresponding with Olson in May of 1962
sending him a letter written in red marker:
"Charles Olson
Here are issues #1 & 2 of new mag we are putting out.
Wd like to know if you would be interested in contributing.
Issue #3 to come out shortly.
Sincerely,
Ed Sanders
Box 193 Stuyvesant Station
New York City."

I mailed him further issues in June, August and October '62
asking for poems to publish
        adding a note to the October letter:

                "Max from Dogtown— I executed
                a forced march on my mind.
                One of poems to always come back to.

                to publish.

                Some work of yours for Fuck You/ 5 ?
                #5 with Marchall/Wieners/Bremser....
                Zap!
                Ed Sanders"

Finally Olson sent "three poems from the Maximus Poems"!
which I published in #5, Vol 1, Dec. '62

On July 8, 1963 I wrote him:
"....Wept the whole mid-day over
'As the Dead Prey Upon Us,' plus Ginzas
poem to Joan Burroughs in *Reality Sandwiches.*
Wieners still weak and shaky after his hepatitis
though beaming in the Cobra Barge as ever....
I'll miss the Vancouver stomp, unfortunately: money,
time and the like. I hope someone from the East makes
tapes/films etc. Have commissioned a report
from a spaceout [Carol Bergé] who is headed there."

On 8-16-63 sent O the freshly published
    Poem from Jail:

"Charles,
Hope this not to
you what Ginzap
calls the 'beatnik
yak-yak.' Anyway
I was 21, in jail,
& with a bunk's
length of toilet paper
morning   afternoon
and evening   Plus my
Egyptian Grammar for which
I had to fast since the
jailers thot it a
Russian code book.
Hoping this finds thee well
& the scorpions out of
the flesh.

zap
Ed Sanders."

At NYU
    in my final year before graduating, in 1964,
    majoring in Greek, I translated just about all 1022 lines
        of Hesiod's *Theogony*
        inspired by Hesiod's lines
            cited in "Maximus from Dogtown— I"

    He sent "West Gloucester, a Maximus Letter"
    in early '64 which I published
    in #5, Volume 7 in August of '64
                      "The God Issue"

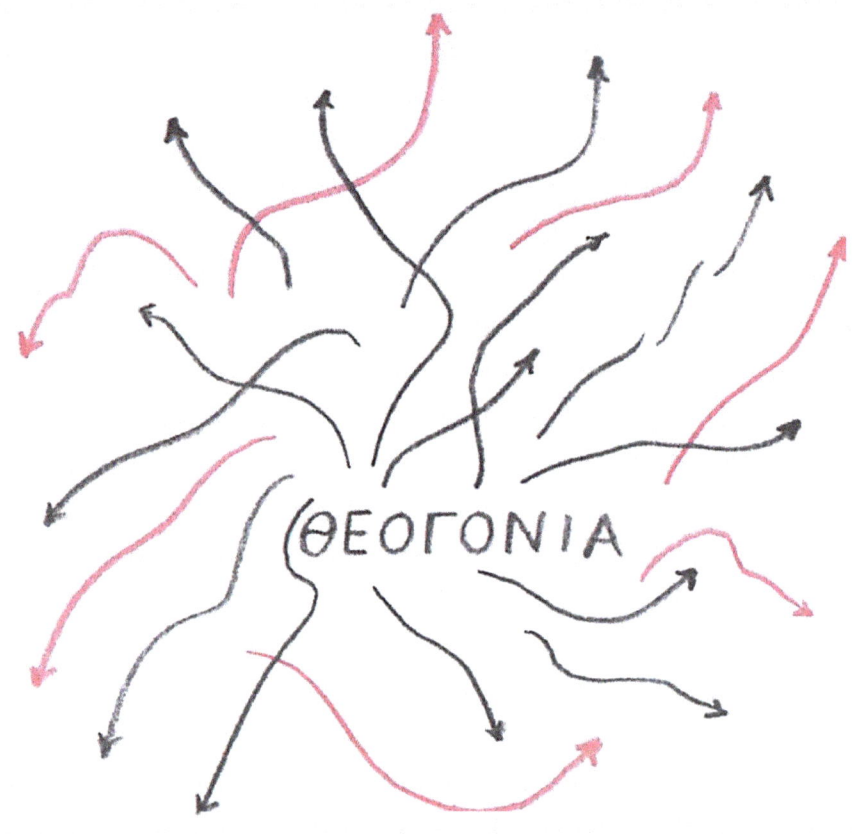

The Theogony

O to University at Buffalo

1963-fall of '65

O flew to the Vancouver Poetry Conference
                          the summer of '63
He, Phil Whalen and Allen Ginsberg
        stayed at the home of Warren & Ellen Tallman

    Olson's 4-hour closing reading on August 16
        was very well received
    w/ O telling Betty it was the best reading he'd ever given

    His pay: $900
        which he could really use

At the Vancouver conference
Olson was offered a distinguished professorship
at the newly founded SUNY Buffalo

by a classics scholar and writer named Al Cook
who'd been brought to SUNY Buffalo
to chair the English Department & organize the writing faculty

The job would begin in just a few weeks
& O, still in Vancouver,
        accepted the offer.

Betty opposed the move very strongly
and refused to go to Buffalo
        though later relented

The three settled into a fairly fancy
"mansion," the Hooker house, in nearby Wyoming

    as O began teaching in the fall of '63
    & quickly attracted a lively and talented
        group of students

Robert Kennedy, campaigning for the U.S. Senate
drew a huge crowd to the Buffalo campus
        10-3-63 at Norton Union

Olson was enthused by the
Black Mountain-ite gathering
of students, followers & listeners

Betty disliked
    being trapped
        in a rural house,
however much a "mansion"
with O, for instance, tarrying with students
        at Onetto's after class

Death of Betty

March 28, 1964

That day Betty drove to the nearby town of Batavia
purchased an Easter basket for Charles Peter
    went to a movie
        then drove on icy roads
            back toward Wyoming
                it was after dark

Her VW crashed into an oncoming truck
        crushing her chest
           unconscious when taken to the hospital
        where she passed away
               not quite 39

She resided in an open casket in the house
        while Olson shook over her
               with enormous grief

It was just 10 years after Betty
        had performed Stepan Wolpe's setting
        of a song from *Peer Gynt*
                at Black Mountain

Later Charles Peter
        was taken to the care of Betty's sister
           Jean Radoslovich

Spring 1964

Olson roamed
the site of
Betty's
    fatal
    crash
looking to
    clearly discern
what had happened

worried
    she had killed
        herself
& that he'd not
cared for her enough
        in person

All the Remnants, fragments, & jottings —

Such as Olson's writing on a copy of John Wieners' Ace of Pentacles

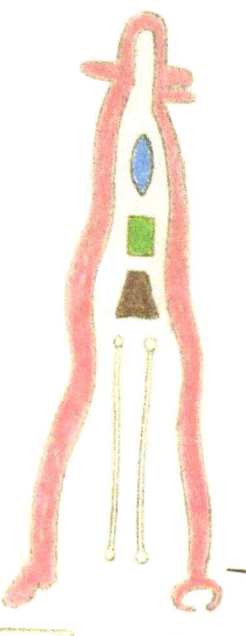

On October 9, '64 reading John Wieners book, "Ace of Pentacles" Charles Olson wrote three short "Poems on Bet" 2 of them jotted upon the pages of "Pentacles" — His mate Betty Kaiser had died in a car crash 3-28-64. These 3 poems were left out of the final volume of Maximus.

(Thanks to Luke Franklin's article on O's marginal inscriptions on "Pentacles")

Poems for Bet

I went full tilt
And then she was killed,
in her automobile

      I need every bleeding minute now
I don't have any time for any new life

          reading John Wieners'
          Ace of Pentacles, Friday
          October 9th 1964

    Friday,
    October 9th
    Nineteen
    Sixty-
    Four   Follow Bet
    Into
    The colors of her dress
    and up the weak ladder
    to the
    Face of God

Bet 2

Her skin
covered me, let light into me, held
my nature, kept me
for myself, and I wasn't sorry
to be closer. In the horrors and transparent
policy,
of the present...

The typescript just above, "Bet 2," was typed
by O same night of 10-9-64, created from
the lines below, which he wrote in
Ace of Pentacles:

Stay close
to her, at no matter what cost.
She is—she was, she does cover
your soul . . .

Charles Peter in '64

After Betty's horrible accident
Olson attempted to keep their son Charles Peter
            by his side

but that became impossible
so he was placed in the care of Betty's sister
Jean Radoslovich and her husband, in Gloucester

That fall of '64 Charles Peter
        attended a Catholic school
& had his first communion at Christmastime
        at Our Lady of Good Voyage

with his father in attendance.

As Ἡροδότου of Halicarnassos

I would be an historian as Herodotus was, looking for himself for the evidence of what is said...

      Maximus I
      Letter 23

Dorcester fishermen (just arrived)
took over a Pilgrim-built
fishing stage
      in Gloucester 1623-24
& Plymouth-men (Myles Standish)
came to fight over it
      the next year

Olson describes it:

> What we have in this field in these scraps among these fishermen, and the Plymouth men, is more than the fight of one colony with another, it is the whole engagement against (1) mercantilism (cf. the Westcountry men and Sir Edward Coke against the Crown, in Commons, these same years—against Gorges); and (2) against nascent capitalism except as it stays the individual adventurer and the worker on share—against all sliding statism, ownership getting in to, the community as, Chambers of Commerce, or theocracy; or City Manager

Harvey Brown & Olson

He was Harvey Brown III
    27 in 1964
He had inherited a lot of money
& had been raised in Cleveland

where, very young, he had grown
fascinated with jazz
       and had founded a recording company
           to help artists such as Don Cherry, Ornette Coleman,
                   Clifford Brown and Clifford Jordan

Harvey was what you could call "shy/bold"
& filled a number of notebooks with his own poetry
       but was very shy about it

He was living in Cambridge with Polly Jones
whose father was the head of
        Harvard U Press

(They were married late in '64)

Harvey stayed with Jack Clarke
in Buffalo a few weeks in the fall of '64
       while he audited Olson's courses

He founded *Niagara Frontier Review*
& soon, inspired & prodded by O
      formed Frontier Press
         which between '66 & '71 brought out
         25 books and pamphlets

(one of the first was my *Peace Eye*, with an intro by O)

(His economic support of O
in the mid-late '60s
    you could say, made it more possible
    through the banishment of penury-worry

for O to write the poems, '65-'69
       in *Maximus III*)

Some books on the Frontier Press Book Boat

Spring Arts Festival in Buffalo

Early April, 1965

I flew to Buffalo to take part in the Spring Arts Festival,
which included visiting Charles Olson's classes, and giving a
poetry reading with Olson and John Wieners at the Student Union.

Olson had invited Wieners, his student at Black Mountain College,
to join him in Buffalo

Wieners, born in Boston, had a degree from Boston University,
and his book, *The Hotel Wentley Poems*, had made a big impression
on the poets of my generation.
I had met him in 1962 when he worked at the Eighth Street Bookshop,
and I published him several times in *Fuck You/ A Magazine of the Arts*.

From U. of Buffalo Student Newspaper, April 9, 1965

I stayed in Buffalo with the Curator of the Lockwood Memorial Library
Poetry Collection, David Posner & his then-wife.

While visiting Olson's class I was thrown for a semi-loop
when he asked me in front of the group
to expound on his conept of
"Topos/Typos/Tropos."

All Hail to the Rebel Cafe!

They gathered after Olson's classes
'63 – into '65

his students
    plus O himself
    plus, for a while
    Gregory Corso
openly puffing on a joint

& Olson lighting up some
    "Asthmador" cigarettes
      containing stramonium &
        belladonna
to mask the pot –

O commenting that Gregory
"was going to blow us all
    out of Buffalo"

~ALL HAIL
  Onetto's
    in Buffalo!!

Corso Refuses to sign Loyalty Oath
Spring 1965

Around the time of the Spring Arts Festival of April '65 the bard
Gregory Corso was required to sign the so-called Feinberg certificate
certifying that he was not then
a member of the Communist Party—
& if he had ever been, to fess up
to the University

The Feinberg text reads:

"Anyone who is a member of the Communist Party or of any organization
that advocates the violent overthrow of the Government of the United States
or of the State of New York or any political subdivision thereof cannot be
employed by the State University. Anyone who was previously a member
of the Communist Party or of any organization that advocates the violent
overthrow of the Government of the United States
or of the State of New York or any political subdivision thereof
is directed to confer with the President before signing this certificate. [...]
This is to certify that I have read the publication of the University of the State
of New York, 1959, entitled Regents Rules on Subversive Activities together
with the instructions set forth above and understand that these rules and
regulations as well as the laws cited therein are part of the terms
of my employment. I further certify that
I am not now a member of the Communist Party
and that if I have ever been a member of the Communist Party
I have communicated that fact to the President of the State
University of New York."

Less than a month after the Spring Arts Festival
Corso was fired by the University
because he refused to sign the loyalty oath

In response, there was a protest picket
held by the Faculty-Student Committee for Academic Freedom,
as reported in the University of Buffalo student newspaper:

The Festival of Two Worlds

Late June '65

Olson and John Wieners
        (also Lawrence Ferlinghetti, John Ashbery, & others)

flew to Italy to read at the prestigious Festival of Two Worlds
                                      at Spoleto.

Olson's Black Mountain comrade Ben Shahn
                created the festival's poster

It gave a chance to read poetry in the presence of the ever-silent Ezra Pound
O hadn't seen Lb since the 1940s
    (when he had visited him in D.C. some 24 times)

Introduced by John Ashbery at his reading
    (with O's reading followed by those of
                Bill Berkson and Pier Paolo Pasolini)

O then intoned "The Song of Ullikummi"
                to Pound who was seated in the royal box.

After the reading, at an outdoor café
        O expounded on something I had written to him,
        about a vision of Pound at 80, embarking on a
                "revival of life and 15 further years of power."

Pound replied, "Sanders has a sense of humor"

John Wieners sent me a postcard from the Festival on June 29:

Dear Eddie
    This is where we read from.
It is quite fun and very elegant.
We stay in an 8 room hotel, just
opened, commanding full
valley view and aquaduct
built in 13th c, still white snow.
All are here, except Allen who refused, and I
miss him. And you too. What a place
to freak their brains.
        Love,
          John
Ezra arrives Tomorrow

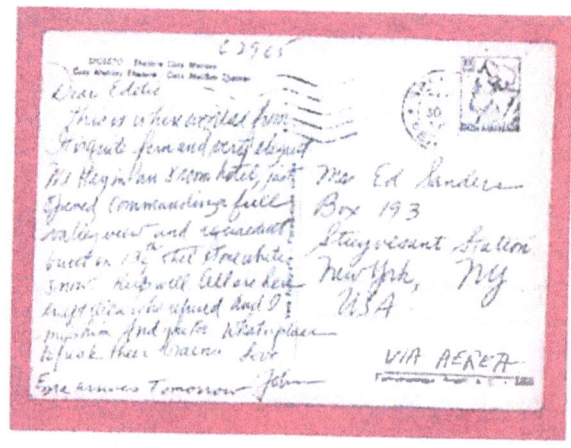

6.29.65

SPOLETO - Théâtre Caio Melisso
Caio Melisso Theatre · Caio Melisso Theater

Dear Eddie,
This is where we read from. It is quite fun and very elegant. We stay in an 8 room hotel, just opened, commanding full valley view and aqueduct built in 13th ctl. Stone white snow. Keep well. All are here except Allen who refused. And I miss him. And you too. What a place to freak their brains. Love

Ezra arrives tomorrow. John

Mrs. Ed Sanders
Box 193
Stuyvesant Station
New York, NY
USA.

VIA AEREA

The Berkeley Poetry Conference July 12-24, 1965

In July Allen, O, Dorn, Creeley et al flew to SF
        for the Berkeley Poetry Conference
one of those gatherings
    whose impact ripples out through
      decades in the world of
           poesy & theory–

Gary Snyder, Robert Creeley,
Jack Spicer (who would pass away soon after), Robert Duncan
John Wieners, the great Charles Olson
plus some of us (then) younger bards:
Ted Berrigan, Lenore Kandel, and myself

(Donald Allen, editor of the *New American Poetry* anthology,
arranged for Grove Press to fly me out
      —many thanks to Grove Press, which I too casually
        forgot formally to thank all those years ago)

Flew from NY. Took a series of buses to City Lights books.
    "Are you Mr. Sanders of Fuck You/ Press?"
        Yes. "Claude Pelieu is in Room 32 in the basement.
           He is expecting you."

Ginsberg read to a huge crowd in Wheeler Auditorium
where, later in the week, Charles Olson
      gave a genius-level Bacchic talk
        that astounded many
           & left some confused.

It made a kind of legendary impression
this Conference
      featuring talks and readings by Robin Blaser, Robert Creeley,
      Ed Dorn, Richard Duerden, Robert Duncan, Allen Ginsberg,
      Joanne Kyger, Ron Loewinsohn, Charles O, Gary Snyder, Jack
      Spicer, George Stanley, Lew Welch, John Wieners.

Wow.

I flew out to take part in what was billed as a "Special Reading"
with Ted Berrigan, John Sinclair and Lenore Kandel

At the Conference I took the opportunity
        to spend as much time with Creeley, Dorn
        and especially Olson as I could

    One of my fellow readers
    at the Poetry Conference
    said not long after
    that I had followed Olson around
                like a puppy

    It's so! I glued myself
    as much as I could
        to the great O!

    I'd visited him in Gloucester
    w/ Panna Grady, George Kimball and George MacBeth
    & I had read with him and Wieners in Buffalo
    & published him aplenty in my magazine

    so I was very happy to be a glue-shoe.

I would run into Olson and other poets
in Robbie's Cafeteria
        near the Berkeley campus

One afternoon at Robbie's Olson and I had lunch.
He talked about "The Song of Ullikummi"

It was during the afternoon
after his morning lecture, "Causal Mythology,"
during which he spoke about Ullikummi,
                the god of the Diorite Stone
in a Hittite "Theogony" text he'd found in
The Journal of Cuneiform Studies.

He'd read his translation from
    "The Song of Ullikummi"
    at the Spoleto Festival
    from which he'd just
               returned

He wrote it specially
to read w/ Ezra Pound in the audience

(O'd been the first poet to visit Ez at
St. Elizabeth's back in '46)

While we were talking I visited the upstairs bathroom at Robbies
where I magic-markered "Ra is Hip to it All"
           above the mirror

He later spotted my exhortation
to the solar deity in the lavatory
I think he appreciated my love of Egyptian hieroglyphs
in the glyphs I drew for my magazine
   a new issue of which I had brought to Berkeley
  & now I create a fuller version
  of my magic-markered exhortation of 1965:

When I returned, I asked him to write down the full title and publisher
of the Hittite "Song of Ullikummi"

He hand-adorned a sheet of paper
        which I have saved to this day:

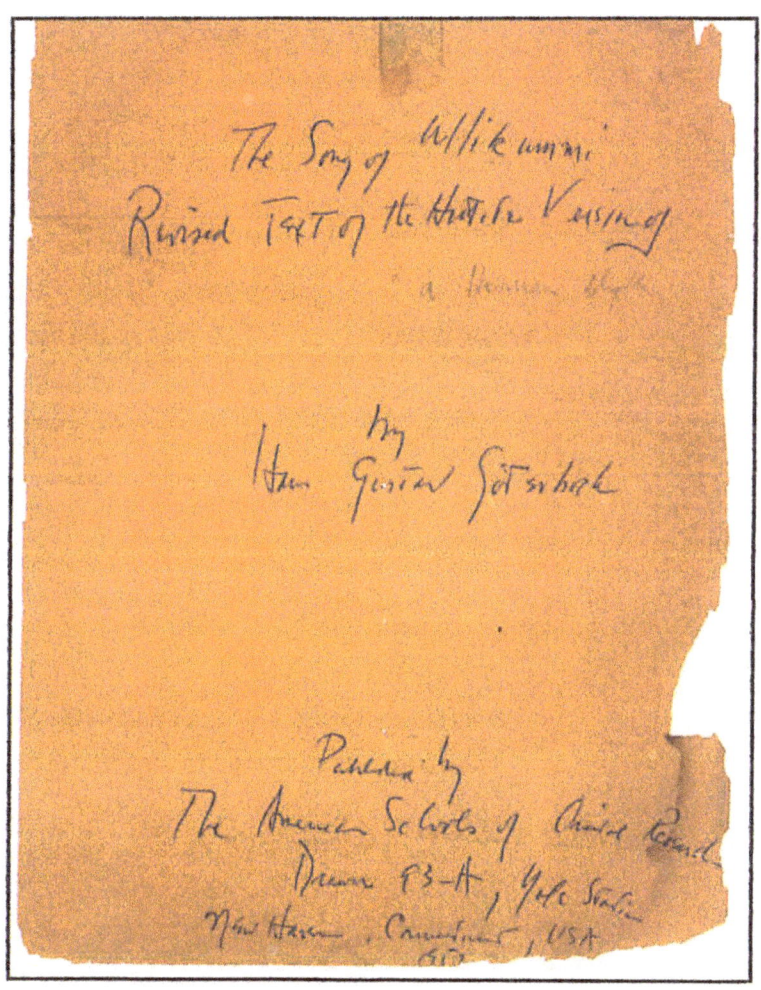

THE SONG OF ULLIKUMMI
REVISED TEXT OF THE HITTITE VERSION OF A HURRIAN MYTH
Hans Gustav Güterbock
Oriental Institute, University of Chicago
Journal of Cuneiform Studies 1951

    Kumarbi
    Pater of the Gods
    balls the mountain

        & creates a Stone Man (Ullikummi)
        to fight agains Enlil, the Storm God

        A story featuring
        the Hurrian deity Kumarbi
        who fathered
                upon a rock cliff
        a genderless, blind
        yet sentient
                pillar of volcanic rock:
                Ullikummi

        —the story pressed in Hittite on clay tablets
        of varying sizes.

Olson described it in the lecture, "Causal Mythology" which
he'd given the morning before our meeting at Robbie's Cafeteria.

In the lecture he'd read four poems written
as O says, "in a run"
                about 1964
"from the Maximus."

and in the course this reading the lines:
        "the Wall
    to arise from the River, the Diorite Stone
    to be lopped off the Left Shoulder"

Bobbie Creeley, in the audience, broke into the Flow to ask
"What do you mean by 'The Diorite Stone lopped
off the Left Shoulder'?"

O's reply: "It's called 'The Song of Ullikummi,'
and it's the story of how this aborted creature, whom the poem calls
the Diorite Stone, starting growing from the bottom of the sea, and
grew until he appeared above the surface of the water, then, of course,
attention was called to him, and he continued to grow, and he became so
offensive to the gods, and dangerous, that they had to themselves do
battle with him; and 'The Song of Ullikummi' is actually the story
of that battle and who could bring him down. Because he had a growth

principle of his own, and it went against creation in the sense that nobody could stop him and nobody knew how far he might grow. It's a marvelous Hesiodic poem. In fact, I prefer it to those passages in Hesiod that include the battle of Zeus with the giants.... because this creature is nothing
but a blue stone...."

—from *Causal Mythology,* July 20, 1965

Later I cross-checked Olson's poem from
"The Song of Ullikummi"
against Güterbock's transliteration &
line by line translation of the original tablets:

The Song of Ullikummi

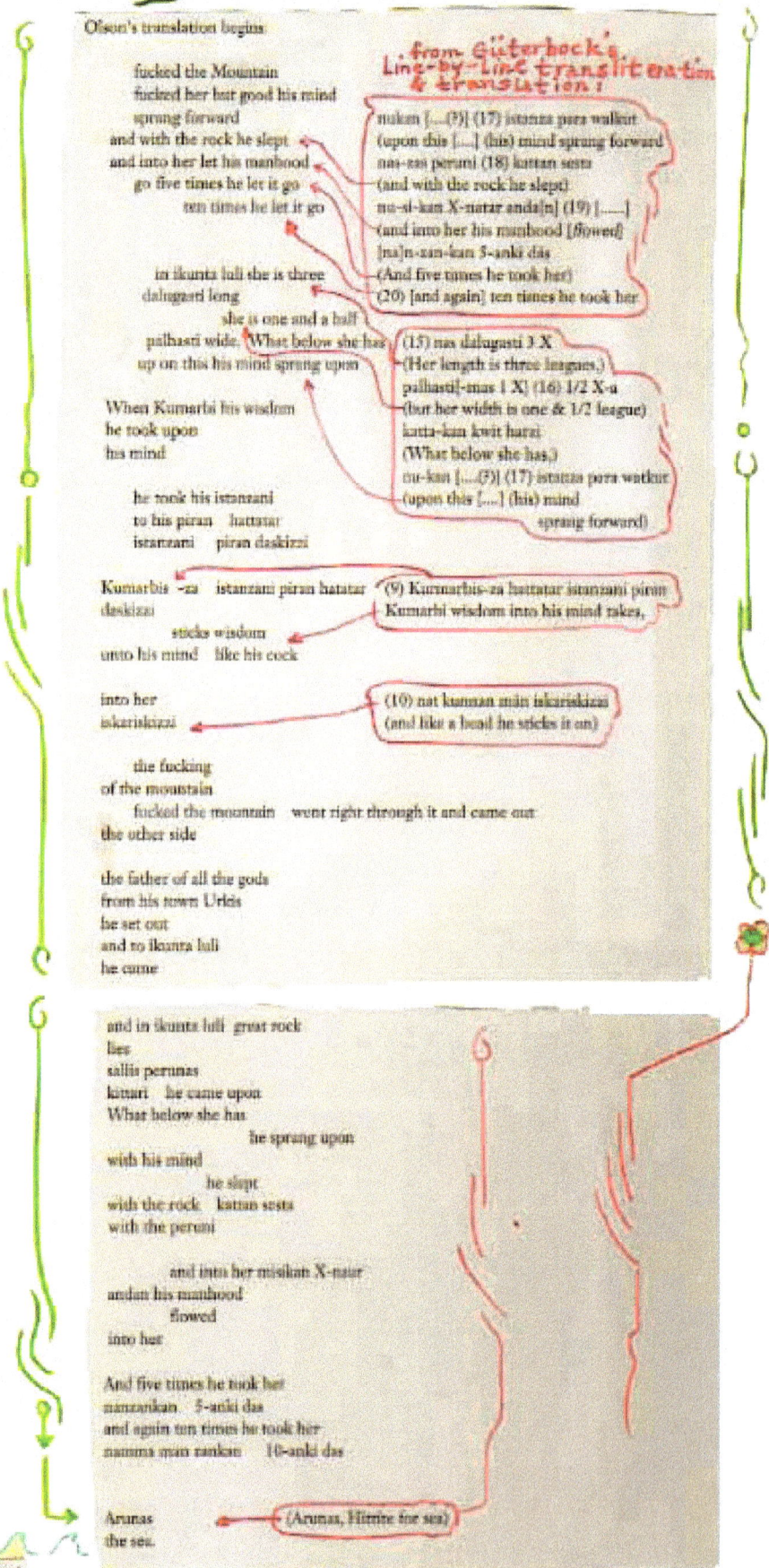

1965

a fine poem
to have read for Pater Pound
            in Spoleto!
(whom O started reading
      in early '45
            from Ernest Hemingway's own library.

"Don't Get Stuck in Europe — Head for Hittite Country"

When Robin Blaser left Boston for Europe on a freighter
July 14, 1959

    Olson came to the ship
            to wish him bon voyage

    and gave Blaser the 1850 1st edition
    of *Redburn: His First Voyage*

    & just before leaving the ship, said to Blaser:

        "Don't get stuck
                in Europe

        Head for Hittite country"

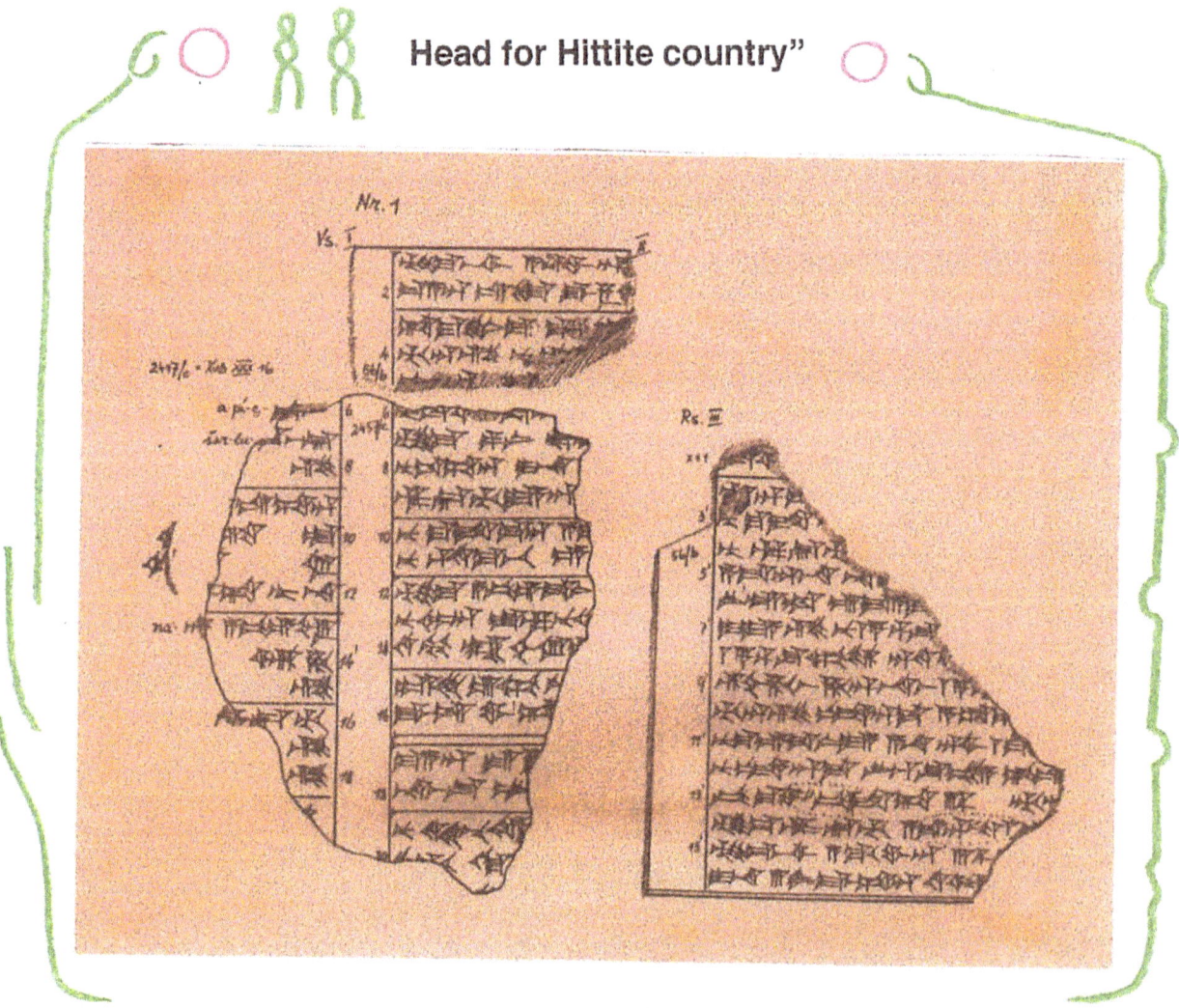

Olson's Reading the Evening of July 23, 1965

In the early evening
Olson and his new friend Susanne
(whom apparently he had met at the Conference)
        and I walked
            across the campus to Wheeler Auditorium
                the site of O's reading/lecture

We strolled past Carl Sauer's house on the Berkeley Campus
He pointed it out in praise.

Then we entered Wheeler Auditorium,

His talk was the stuff of legend.

Olson was lorn for love,
as when during the Conference he fell in love
with a young participant named Suzanne, and
hoped to elope with her after his reading
July 23, 1965 at Wheeler Auditorium

In the middle of O's recitations she sent me a message
written on the inside of a match book:

> "Ed: he asked
> (Charles) me to
> marry him & he's
> SERIOUS and
> he thinks we are
> getting married
> after this, <u>tonight</u>
> in Arizona and I
> CAN'T, and have
> to run away; can
> you hlp me, tell
> me what to say,
> or should I just
> leave?"

        I quickly jotted a note back

suggesting that she sit tight; that
the others, including Ginsberg, Dorn,
Wieners, Creeley understood what was going on.

Olson had told her the previous night
she wrote me

"All my boys have gotten ahead of me"

and that Olson had no new poems

and, as she jotted to me,
"no huge group here as
compared with say, Ginsberg and even Creeley
who really brought them in. And he was so scared,
and feeling good, as though he would (maybe)
do good, that I couldn't tell him this morning
that I couldn't marry him. And he's renting a
house and car, and phoned the marriage bureau
etc etc. And I'm going crazy. I mean
I love him, but I love you too, and Dave, and Creeley
and oh— the young boys with their casual bodies.....

**I retrieved O's Cutty Sark
bottle from the lectern after his reading**

The Beach Wagon of Eternity

Departing Buffalo back to Gloucester

After two weeks of classes the fall of '65
    Olson decided to depart his professorship
        and return to Gloucester

To ward off the Mallet of Pov
Harvey set up a $20,000 annual payment
    to O as an advisor to Frontier Press.

(When O left home in the fall of '69 to lecture at UConn
    he had placed a bunch of penury-banning $5,000 checks
        from Harvey Brown, uncashed
            in a deposit box in a Gloucester bank)

O's Beach Wagon

Jack Clarke excitedly later described driving
O's beach wagon
    absolutely filled with
      his books and papers from
          Buff' to Glou'

but on the way
the wagon caught a-fire
      & was ruined

but realizing how much affection
O had for this vehicle
    Clarke looked in lots
    till he bought for $300
    the same-hued look-alike
        wagon
then packed it w/ O's archive
    & brought it
        to Fort Square

This photo by Ann Charters in '68 I think is of O's Beach Wagon parked near 28.

When Charles Boer visited Gloucester in '69
he drove the Beach Wagon out for some sandwiches
        & discovered the reverse was out

    Too bad O's wagon wasn't preserved
        in his Archive.

Homeric Ship

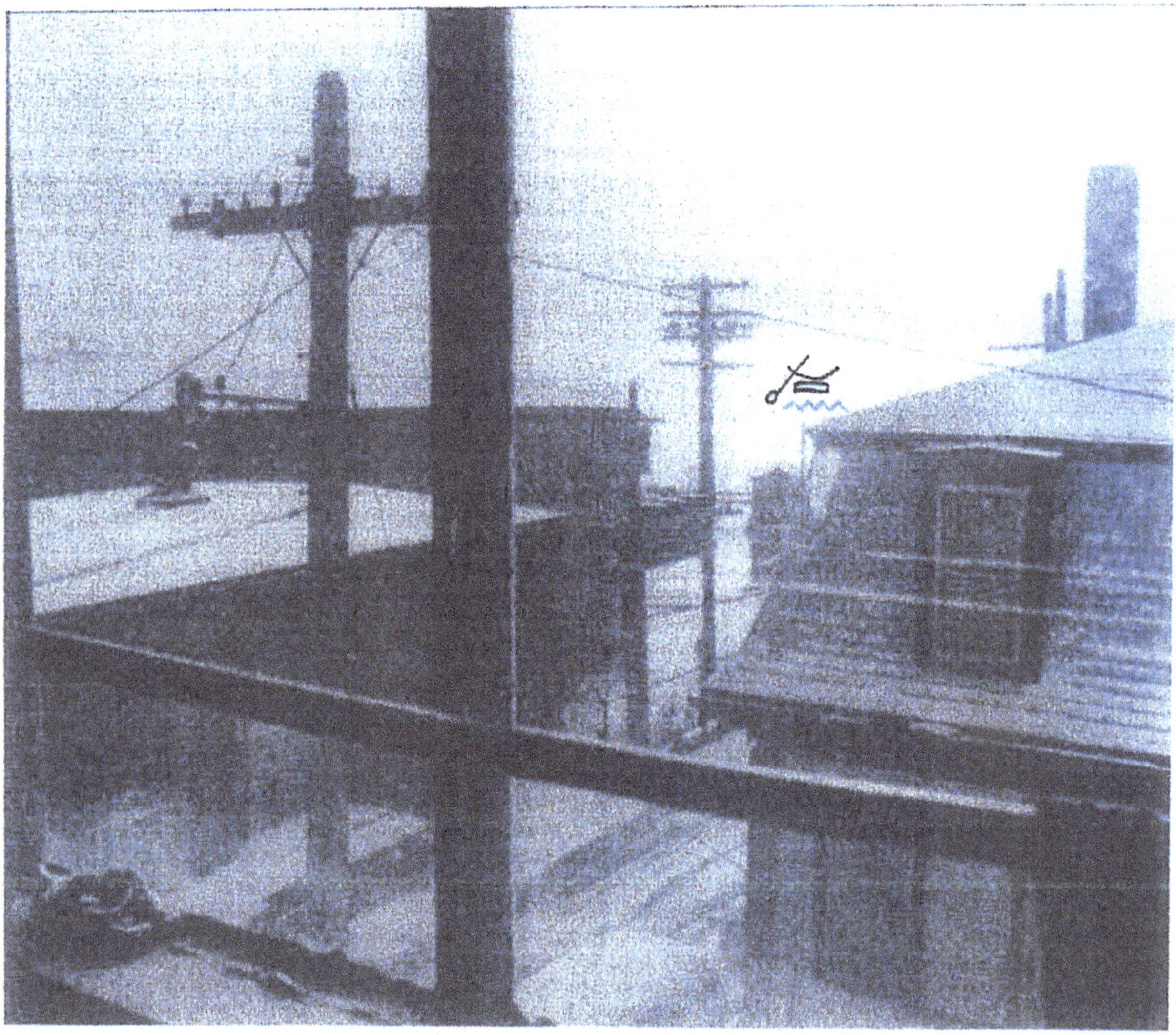

Looking out the
Window
at
28 Fort Square

Letters to Olson, housed at the UConn Library
Late '65-early '66

Nov 9, 1965
Los Angeles

"Dear Charles---
Well, the Fugs have been on a coast to coast concert tour— stayed in the Berkeley-S.F. area for three weeks. Ginzap was on a couple of concerts with us— the Zap is now billed as Folk Rock Mantra-ist. We are on the way to the Creeley conspiracy in Placitas. Traveling w/ wife, daughter Deirdre, and the 4 other Fugs. It's been a great month touring, although I sometimes feel like I'm traveling with Albanian hillsmen storming Byzantine nunneries.

"Ginsberg, with the Orlovsky brothers, in the microbus soon to travel around the states. Michael McClure writing Rock Message Units for the local S.F. singing groups. He and Ginzap & Bruce Conner practicing daily on rhythm mantras. Some of it pretty good. Why don't you write a song for the Fugs: Olson message to the young & humm the tune into a tape recorder— send tape and text. We're done a lot of Blake: Ah Sunflower Wearing of Time; How Sweet I Roamed from Field to Field; Oh Rose Thou Art Sick; Swinburne Stomp (a chorus from *Atalanta in Calydon* "Before the Beginning of Years.), Ginzap, etc.

'2 days later--
Now at Creeleys'. Extremely hospitable, kind, generous. 6 fug maniacs on the Placitas set. Now to the real reason of letter.

A very elegant lady on the N.Y. literary scene with a large opulently furnished apartment at the Dakota on 72nd and C. Park West, living alone, I believe an Esterhazy countess with Rockefeller money, has on several occasions mentioned interest in having you stay with her for a while— to meet you, etc. She has a maid or two-- incredible apartment. (I filmed part of mongolian cluster fuck there) very large with lots of phones & whole sections I'm sure you could be alone in.

"She's an excellent cook the type who'll spend 8 hours making Hungarian horse radish with income from scads of stocks— she entertains on the highest social levels & throws the most interesting of the N.Y. literary in-bashes. Why don't you bop in to N.Y. and spend some time there. I'd be glad to like handle any details, arrange the date, or help in whatever way. In any case, you now have a N.Y. base on the most comfortable level, with $, lots of those Kennedy/Shriver/ freaks all around.

"Send me some poetry for an issue?

How about any prose you may have written, a message from the big O to the young Turks, for the prose issue of F.Y./?

Terrence Williams mentioned with joy and delight that you might freak in to K.U. for a two week scene. The Cree is not too far away— he could come & be someone to talk to, maybe. Let me know if anything I can do in N.Y. for you.

Instant publication of course, of any project you have in mind.

Love,
Ed"

Thursday Dec 2
"Dear Charles, Joy to get all your letters. Called Panna G.
today— she's planning elegant dinner parties for you— you
can stay I hope for a while? Just let me know a few days in advance
so I can set things up. Ok. Thanks for the wonderful piece for F.Y.
Hard to transcribe on the typewriter. I'll send thee a dummy copy
for your proofreading.
Love,
Ed."

December 11, 1965
Charles—
wonderful pictures and poem on the editorial page! I have written to the president of Essex County Newspapers, Philip Weld, to try to obtain 500 copies of the whole editorial page— telling that I would distribute free to "friends of Mr. Olson & those interested in historical preservation."

The Fugs had the world premier of "I Want to Know" (the kernel of the song is the: we drink or break open our veins solely to know from Max. fr. Dogtown.) The crowds love it: essentially some sort of gnostic chant, in the sense there is a terrific <u>Hunger</u> built up in the song from those beginning lines. Hope you not pissed off: but is this insistence on KNOWING that has always intrigued me in that supreme *Maximus from Dogtown*. So we have written to present the message to the kiddies. They love it. Sure to make the top 40, if it comes out on a 45 record....

....Where is the poem presenting the Bundy-Gloucester fish hegemony?

Love,
Ed

P.S. Panna Grady is, indeed on the preparedness scene. All we need is few days notice and not even that."

January 24, 1966
Dear O,
I suppose by now you have heard of my arrest on a F.Y./ porn charge. A.C.L.U. handling the case/ should have very little trouble on appeal, although It'll be tied up in the courts for years.

Now: (a) what's the scene re: Panna? I think John Wieners is freaking in there around this week & then will disappear after the semester break. Anytime you want to bop down, is fine with her. There'll be a huge freak scene for Norman Mailer's new book of essays on the 13th there, so you may or may not want to stomp in for that action. Her # TR 4-7481. 1 W. 72nd Street."

(Then the letter goes on to ask for a signed okay to use his lyrics in "I Want to Know.)

The letter ends: "Yes yes yes please send your further statements for F.Y./ a gala ARREST ISSUE is being produced, and your material will provide that eternal weight to make the F.Y. feather fall. Philip Weld of G. Times wrote and said no can supply that poem. So I'll try to reduce the page via photo offset.
Love, Ed."

A Scream to the Editor
December 3, 1965

Olson wrote 17 separate letters to the Gloucester Times
five were poems, and 12 were prose
                      beginning in Dec of '62

He stood against the ravages of so-called "urban renewal"
'gainst the loss of historic architecture
                      & against the filling of wetlands
& the other "erosions of place."

So in December of '65
as I was preparing a new issue of my magazine

      I learned of Olson's
      "Scream to the Editor,"
which had been given nearly an entire page
                    of the *Gloucester Daily Times*

so I tried to arrange with the editor, Philip Weld
to purchase 500 copies
so I could add it to my magazine

but he wrote back
              "Terribly sorry, but the back issues of
              the Times of Dec. 3 with Charles Olson's
              poem were rapidly cleaned out. There's no
              practical way we can supply you with
                          500 copies'

but he did send me the printed page with the letter
which is all I have, over 50 years later,
              a tattered copy in my archive.

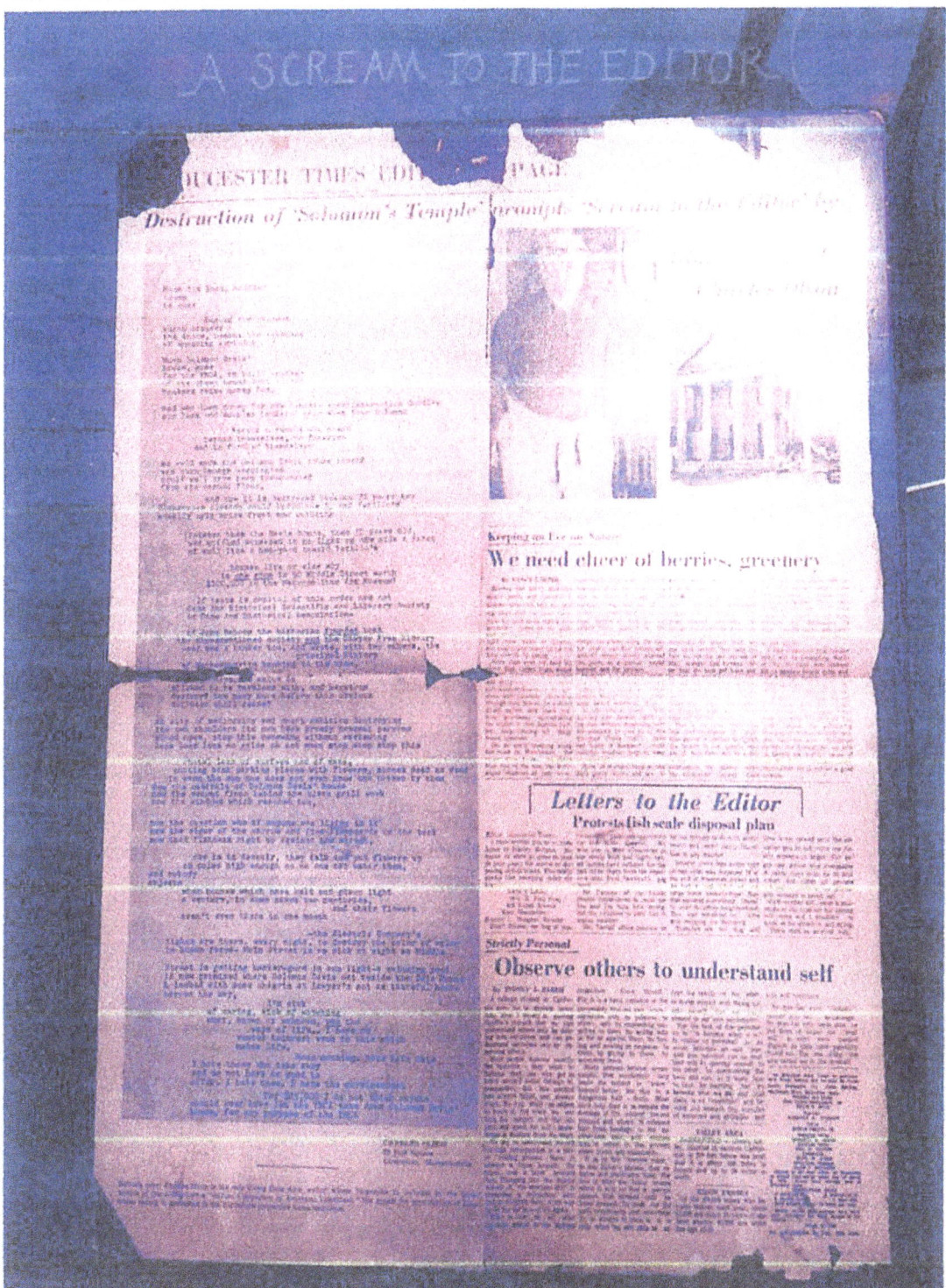

A Scream to the Editor

Moan the loss, another house
is gone
        Bemoan the present
which assumes
its taste, bemoan the easiness
of smashing anything

A Scream to the Editor

Moan the loss, another
house
is gone
          Bemoan the present
which assumes
its taste, bemoan the easiness
of smashing anything

Moan Solomon Davis'
house, gone
for the YMCA, to build another
of its cheap benevolent places
bankers raise money for,

and who loan money for new houses. each destruction doubl
our loss and doubles 'bankers' gains when four columns

  — Gloucester Daily Times
     December 3, 1965

Solomon Davis house
torn down
in Gloucester
in 1965
bemoaned
by Charles Olson

Edward Sanders
March 9, 2018

Raid of Peace Eye Bookstore
January 1, 1966

Peace Eye Bookstore was raided by officers of the
    NYPD 9th Precinct
      I was arrested for obscenity
        & oodles of my magazine & publications
            were carted away by the police

Allen Ginsberg did a benefit for me in L.A.
& the New York Civil Liberties Union
            took on my court defense.

Letters of support came aplenty
    including from Norman Holmes Pearson
            & Edward Dorn
& I lined up John Ashbery & Kenneth Koch as expert witnesses

Letter of Support from O

Charles Olson sent hand-written letter of March 9, 1966;

"Ed   I'd
certainly enjoy seeing you
Get on yr helli-kopter if that's
  what you
      got :

          Try me — (and I'll also
      if I can ever get paper turned
      into

Copy <u>and</u> print you'll have
those 2 or 3 other

Endeavors (of December
        [prose contributions to an issue
        I was putting together late '65]

      Good Lord I <u>always</u>

fear to look at <u>yesterday</u>   because
                                today
—usually— I'm interested
         another way

                   On yr shit & all that
—& Lord yes ...... believe & call on me for
anything: money (?) attestation — +

      (though as you know it would take— Better (?) to
Supreme Court — I can't see how you can
have any trouble at all— but if it is a
mater of <u>your life & freedom Sir</u>
                             I'll
<u>walk</u> to appear in court in Manhattan for
you

             Love

              O

have any trouble at all — but if it is a matter of *your life & freedom, sir*

walk to appear in court in Manhattan for

you love

in the farthest East

Where the sun does in fact come up out of the ocean, curiously

yours

Charles

Snow At Evening

In the twilight snow for less than a minute
less than the time I proposed to write
that the green of the whiting dragger the Santa Lucia
was, two minutes ago, as worn & exact as the color
of that Saint's eyes as they lie as, three minutes ago
the color of the leaden sky too was the pewter of the plate she
holds her eyes out on in Zurbubran's painting of her act of
life & its proposed loss

                    Wednesday January 20th 1966

Olson

Maximus III
p. 488

Saint Lucia
martyr
who was killed
during Diocletianic Persecution

303 Diocletian
published his 1st Edict against the
                              Christians
who were not allowed to assemble
& their scriptures destroyed

till 311

Zurbaran
young girl
holding a gray pewter plate
            w/ 2 eye balls on it
    c 1625/1630
(legend: sent her eyes to a suitor —
sight later brought back to her
during prayer)

Trip to Gloucester
April 1966

The English poet George MacBeth had been staying with Panna
during a trip to the States, and wanted to visit O

    so she reached out to me
    and I set up the visit.

I lined up writer George Kimball who had an auto
so we drove up and back the same day and night

I brought O a gift, a Greek edition of Hesiod's
Theogony, with a French interlinear translation
(O got in touch with me shortly after the visit,
informing me that the *Theogony* I had given him
    contained some of my writing,
        a draft of the "Out of the sea, o Aphrodite"
        section of "Virgin Forest," (just recorded)
        on the Fugs Second Album.

Kimball: "The car was some kind of off-green Ford wagon
I'd bought in Colorado (it had belonged to Peggy Fleming's father)....
We had some kind of
    mechanical problem en route... Whatever it was

I had no idea how to fix it, but you apparently did,
    just opened the hood, did some mumbo jumbo
    and told me to start it again and it worked."

    (I stood upon the fender, opened the hood and reached
        down into the engine, & primed the carburetor
        and beckoned to Kimball
        to try it again, and it started)

We had dinner at The Tavern followed
    by a walk with Olson on the beach by the harbor

        The O swept his arm across the vista
        and asked, "You know what built Gloucester?"

    Then answered, "Cod!"

Panna Rents House in Gloucester
Summer 1966

Panna Grady moved in
       with her young daughter
to a stone "mansion"
in Riverdale
       on the edge of Dogtown

The "Dennison House"
          as it was known.

John Wieners
       was on hand
             & they were lovers

Psilocybin in Gloucester
early October 1966

The Fugs were enjoying a sold-out run at the
Players Theater on MacDougal Street.

Monday's were our days off
so I flew on the Eastern Shuttle to Boston
with Ken Weaver
       & took a cab to Gloucester
                to visit Olson

Panna Grady was not on hand,
so Olson drove us to the stone house
she had rented on the edge of Dogtown.

First we had a visit to 28 Fort Square
He cleared away some books from the stove-top
to make us some tea
& he was using the Black Mountain seal-stamping device
                         as a door stop
   Then we went out to dinner

Then we were sitting in the kitchen at Fort Square.
We were to stay in the house rented by Panna Grady
      near Dogtown Commons. (She was not there that night.)

Olson had a bottle of orange-red psilocybin pills, plus a bottle,
literally, of Acid he'd gotten from Tim Leary.
He went into a back room and returned with the bottles of
                      LSD and 'cybin.

"Want a swig?" he said, thrusting the liquid acid my direction,
as if it were a shot of rum in a Gloucester

"A swig!!" I exclaimed knowing full well that 350-500 micrograms
was more than enough— why should we risk some
    500,000 microgram gulps? so we settled on the psilocybin.

Olson shook out a handful of red orange pills. I took about 8—
Weaver as I recall had 12, and Olson, at 6 foot 7,

had an initial 12 or so, then a few more. We sat talking in the kitchen
    while the Mageia 'Shrooms
        began to bring us into the Galaxy.

Then Olson drove us over near the stone house
where we were to sleep. He drove slowly, so slowly that when I
looked back behind a line of cars was close pressed behind us.

He pulled over, as I recall to let some of them roll by, then we proceeded.
I felt a great surge of confidence that my mentor, the O, was driving,
and he would get us there safely. Then I glanced to the front seat,
and Olson had turned into the Greek god Poseidon! literally!
    The Horse from the Sea! with kelp in his mane matted and wet.

So onward drove Poseidon —the seat cushions washed in the froth
of his greeny mane, which seemed ornamented with sea wrack, bone bits,
shells and oceanic oddments! I thought, well even if I am bonkers,
the driver, my hero, my guru, my bard was Safety Assured!

Until we passed a clump of what appeared to be boulders,
in the gloom to the left.
    "Woooo, look at the elephants!" Poseidon shouted.

At last we arrived at the stone house, with stone-arched doorway
and sat in the living room to talk.

Meanwhile, the psilocybin was having a profound effect on me.
It seemed as if the house had become the Chapel Perilous,
    and I began to walk outdoors, spend a few minutes in the dark,
then return back to the Chapel. I did this a few times and seemed to live
through life cycles as I left the house,
    walked through the woods, then returned

        I had no idea at the time
        that I was living through life-cycles
            & returning to the Chapel Perilous
        that O himself was re-experiencing
            in Panna Grady's rented living room
        his first experience with magic mushrooms
                in Dec of '59

        As O later described it:
        "(T)he first time I went under the mushroom
        I went into a big all longhouse take. I discovered a great

truth of the Indians of the territory, who discovered the
Longhouse Principle late, as you know. But we don't know
too much in anthropology yet about the history
of the Longhouse
before the Dekanawidah epic. The epic may have
itself been the result of an Indian experience which hadn't
solidified itself before the Longhouse....

"I'm saying that the [psilocybin house] in Newton,
in the mushroom house under the drug, for me
was a longhouse, and I so said, 'My god,' I said,
'here we are. This is longhouse. Let's... oh wonderful,'

like, and we started to improvise."

And this: "I, under the mushroom, was absolutely
a peace sachem, holding, as chief,
a Longhouse Ceremony."

(The Gratwick Tape, November 16, 1963)

28 Fort Square
October '66

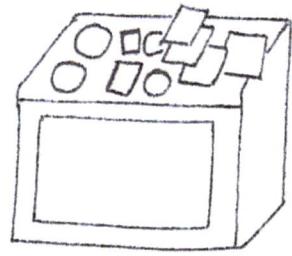

He had to clear some
books off the stove

to make us tea

& he was using
the Black Mountain seal-stamper

as a door stop

The small vial of LSD

"Want a swig?" he said

Want a swig?! I responded

calculating that a "swig" might be what? 25,000 micrograms or more when the recommended hit was like 250-400 micrograms

Driving to Where we were Staying in Gloucester

I felt a great surge of confidence
that my mentor, the O, was driving
and he would get us there safely

Then I glanced to the front seat
and Olson had turned into Poseidon!
literally! the Horse from the Sea!
with kelp on his mane
matted and wet

So on drove Poseidon
— the seat cushions
washed in the froth of his greeny mane
which seemed ornamented with sea wrack,
    bone bits, shells and oceanic oddments!

Psilocybin '66

It seemed as if the Gloucester house
had become the Chapel Perilous,
and I began to walk outdoors
spend a few minutes
then return to the Chapel

I did this a few times and
seemed to live through life cycles
as I left the house, walked through the woods
then returned

Once I spoke Akkadian, building a mud brick hut
by the River Euphrates

In another cycle
I was a Hasidic store owner on Hester Street
                in the Lower East Side

    I told Olson
    the life cycles I was experiencing
    & encounters with the Chapel Perilous

    & he said he preferred to sit
    in the Algonquin Law Lodge

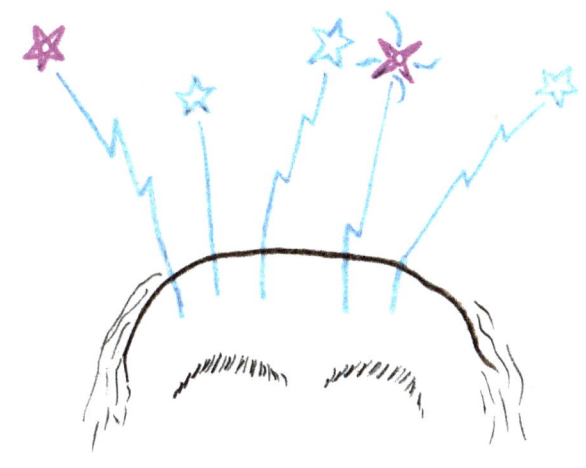

Sparks from
Olson's
forehead
on a
night in
'66

Olson, meanwhile talked onward.
Weaver pointed toward the O:
"Look at those sparks
 coming out of his forehead."
I looked. It seemed
 enormous. This Head-Top
 This Capital
and showering with blue arcs!

The Little Pink Pills

I had no idea at the time
while I was living through life-cycles
    & returning to the Chapel Perilous
that O himself was re-experiencing
    in Panna Grady's rented living room
his first experience with magic mushrooms
        back in Dec of '60.

As O later described it:

"(T)he first time I went under the mushroom
I went into a big all Longhouse take.
truth of the Indians I discovered a great
        of the territory, who discovered
Longhouse Principle late, as you know.

But we don't know
too much in anthropology yet
    about the history

before the Dekanawidah of the Longhouse
        epic.
That epic may have
itself been the result of an Indian Experience
which hadn't solidified itself

        before the Longhouse...
I'm saying that the [psilocybin house] in Newton,
in the mushroom house under the drug, for me
was a Longhouse, and I so said, 'My god,' I said,
'here we are. This is Longhouse... oh wonderful.'"

And Olson said this:
"I, under the mushroom, was absolutely
a peace sachem, holding, as chief,
    a Longhouse Ceremony."

Aces and Eights

Wild Bill was shot in the back
      in a saloon in Deadwood City, South Dakota

   on August 2, 1876
   during a game of five card draw

   with Bill's hand the soon-famous
   Deadman's hand

      —aces and eights

   Olson gave me a
   photo-card of Wild Bill
   during an October '66 visit
      to Fort Square
   when I showed
   ignorance of the phrase
      "Aces & Eights"

Of course   Aces & Eights
is a pretty good hand
      for 5-card draw

which may have been contributory
      to the hot barrel

      —Ed Sanders   August 8, '18

Front Door & Porch
of the Bard
1966 Fort Square

Reading at the 92nd Street YM-YMWHA

A few days after the mushrooms in Gloucester
on October 24, 1966, in the evening, Robert Creeley and John Wieners
read together at the 92nd Street Y.
        I was asked to introduce them
                to the large audience.

      Wieners was very happy at reading, for the first time,
    at such a prestigious place, where T.S. Eliot, W. H. Auden,
e. e. cummings, and other emeralds of poesy plied their bardery in the past.

There was a party at the Chelsea Hotel after the reading
Olson called Bob Creeley at the Chelsea party,
and insisted that Bob hand the phone to John Wieners.

Then O informed Wieners that he and Panna Grady
were traveling to London together. It must have been a blow to John,
and did not reflect well on Olson, who must have known the joy
      Wieners was experiencing that night, reading at the
      awesome 92nd Street Y.

Off to England

October 28, 1966
    Olson, Panna Grady & her young daughter
    sailed from Montreal to Liverpool
                in the *Empress of Canada*

    then to London

O brought his researches and all-night conversations
    to Europe

        meeting with an assortment of poets, friends
                & publishers

Between
the $20,000 a year from Harvey Brown
(about the same as a Guggenheim a year)
plus the largess of
        Panna—

he was free to assume
    a fairly expensive life style

        I received a Christmas card from Panna
        a print by Francescusccio Ghissi
            of the Nativity

        plus hand-written text: "Charles & I
        are taking a lovely big house
            in Regents Park

        for the next half year— So you'll
        have to come visit, plenty of room—
            Come any time.

        The very best for the New Year
        and regards to Ken.

        Love, Panna."

He did write for *Maximus III*, such as
"Out of the Light of Heaven"
        Dec 24, 1966 written in Berlin on
                hotel stationary
where O had been invited to read
    (& another version
    in London 2-28 to 2-23 '67)

and III 179
    "Hotel Steinplatz Berlin
      December 25 (1966)"

where he had a
    mild heart attack
      after which, frightened for his life
        he stayed in bed
          a few days
              in the Hotel Steinplatz

Brown flew over for a visit
& noted he thought the
    O/Grady relationship "was over."

 with various adventures
    till he returned in July '67 to Gloucester
        in time for what they called
            The Summer of Love

The Human Universe
1967

The Human Universe and Other Essays

Bought this 1967 Grove Press edition
(from the '65 Auerhahn Society limited edition)

    late in the year
           while writing & recording the Fugs album
                      Tenderness Junction

    I jotted lyrics
        on pages of *Human Universe*

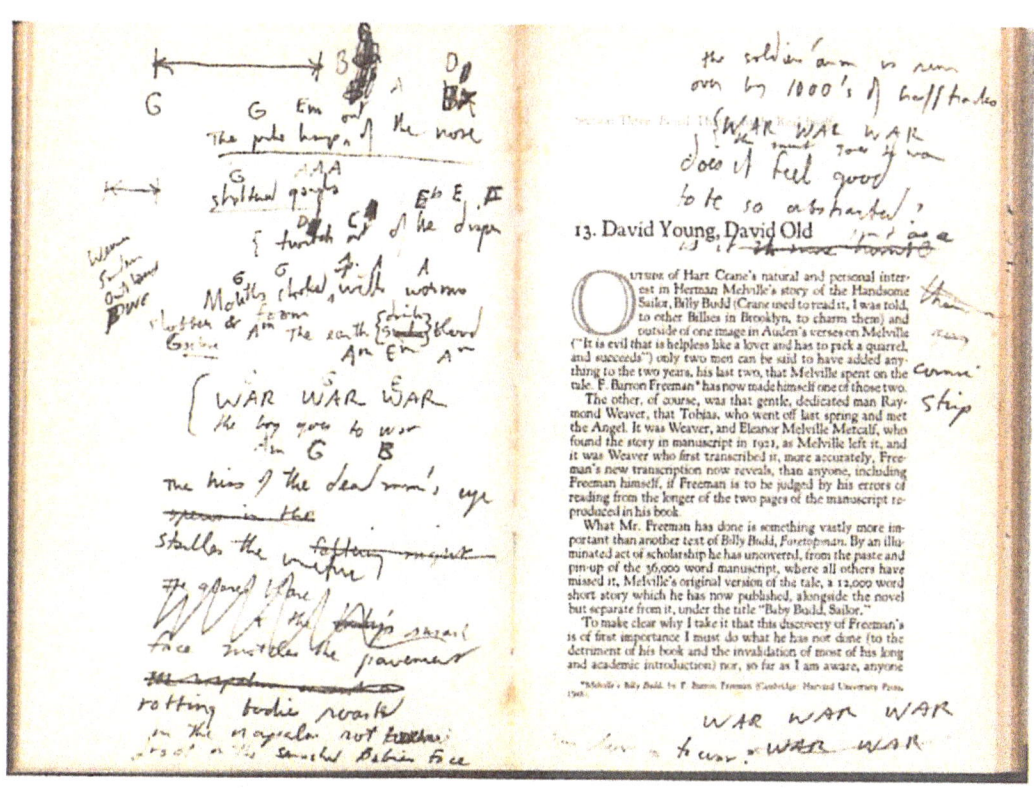

for "War Song" which wound up on the album
such as "WAR WAR WAR
    Does it feel good
    to be so abstracted?
    Is it just as a comic strip?
    WAR WAR WAR
    The boy goes to war."

A Mantram to Chant at the Upcoming Chicago Demonstrations
March 1968

I had written O for a mantram we could chant in Chicago
        to quell the likely violence.
                (and against the war in Vietnam)

I also asked poets Ed Dorn and d.a. levy.
The idea came from the chanting the Fugs and the Diggers
had done at the Pentagon, "Out, Demons, out! Out, Demons, out!"

and the ceremony we had performed with Ginsberg
            at Senator McCarthy's grave.

It was worth a try
        to see if a great bard's sung seed syllables
                could help end the war

On March 14, Charles Olson called Avenue A
            and recited his mantram to Miriam:

> *Plann'd in Creation, Arouse the Nation*
> *Blood is the Food of*
> *Those Gone Mad*
> <u>*Blood is the Food of*</u>
> <u>*Those Gone Mad*</u>
> *Blood is all over already the Nation*
> *Plann'd in Creation, Arouse the Nation*
> *Blood is the Food of Those Gone Mad*

which she jotted down.

He had his bard-eye
        on a big American problem:
                The War Caste wanted blood
                    (then & now)

Olson then mailed us the Chant from Chicago
on the way to deliver some lectures entitled
                "Poetry and Truth" at Beloit College.

Poetry and Truth
1968

    Monday, Wednesday, Friday
              March 25-29, he
    delivered the lectures titled Poetry and Truth
    at Beloit College in Wisconsin

    I was grateful, reading them later,
    that he had expounded in Beloit
    in fairly understandable detail,
    on the terms "topos, typos and tropos"
    from his great essay on poetics
                  "Projective Verse"

For the Beloit lectures
    Olson wrote three short, exquisite poems

two of which ever since
    I have read over and over
        as numinal text

The first I keep in my writing studio
    on the wall
        'neath the Endymion medal from Mardi Gras

the one beginning,
    "an actual earth of value to
      construct one....."

and the "Beloved Lake" poem
beginning,
    "Wholly absorbed
      into my own conduits to
      an inner nature or subterranean lake...."

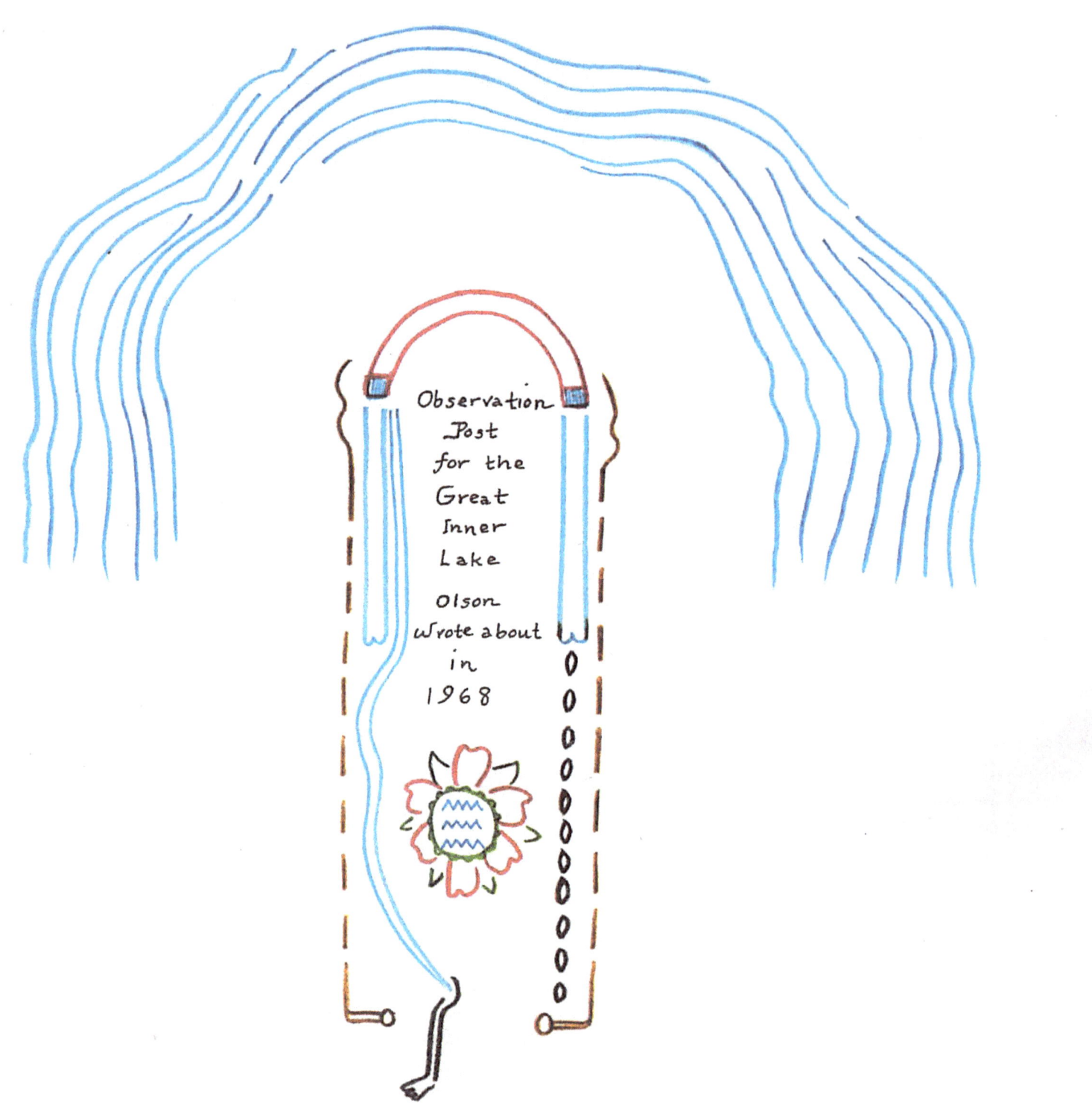

Curriculum of the Soul
1968

Olson drew up a schematic for the
Curriculum of the Soul

the first fascicle (of 29)
    was O's

Trying to set up a Great Poet/Great Singer Romance
1968

I was in San Francisco with the Fugs
in April of 1968
Olson was also in S.F.
staying w/ Don Allen
            after the Beloit Lectures

I knew that my friend Janis Joplin
—living in San Francisco—
was looking for songs for her new album

so I asked her, "Would you like
to meet a great poet?"

She said "Yes."

In addition to the sometimes impecunious bard
placing a tune, or lyrics, on a best seller,

     I thought, well,
     both are single
         so maybe they'd hit it off
            resulting in a great poet/great singer romance

I organized a dinner
at a Chinese restaurant
(paid for by Grove Press!)
w/ me, Ken Weaver, Allen, Janis & Charles

Afterwards we crowded into a booth
            at Gino and Carlo's
                  in North Beach
& I arranged for O and Janis
to sit side by side—
then I heard him mention Sutter's Mill
and the words "Donner Party"
     entered the quick flow of his words.

Around then Janis went to the back
            to shoot pool
    and my plans for
    a blues/bard romance
        were racked up on the green felt.

E.S.
3-21-12

For the Rest of the Life of the Species

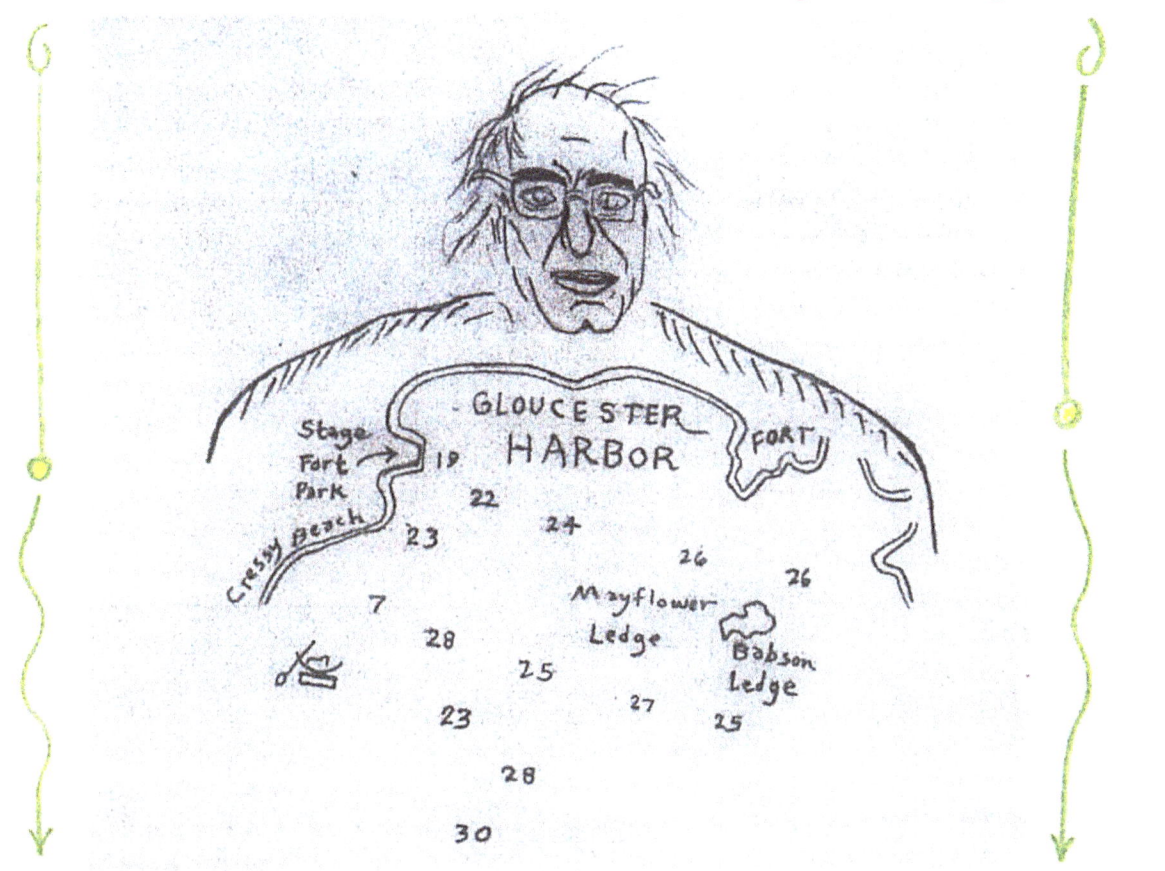

Herb Kenny: Well Charles, what do you think the future of Gloucester and Cape Ann will be?

Olson: An image of creation and of human life for the rest of the life of the species

—Olson talking w/ Herb Kenny Late August '69

Olson Protecting Gloucester

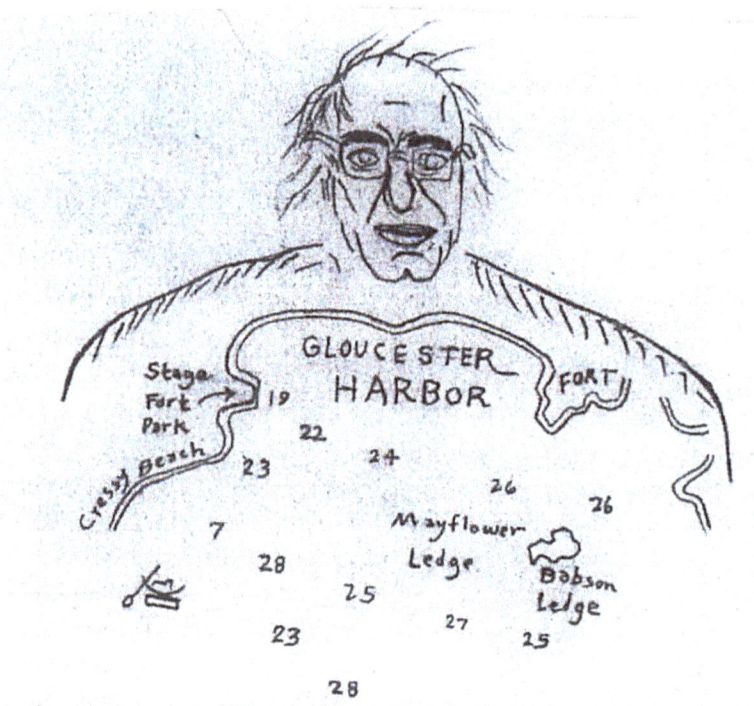

πόλις

"You can never lose to the City Council if your case is Love"

"I even helped in that marsh fight over on Essex Ave... The state refused the permit, happily, because of some aquarian life... they claimed... might be destroyed."

—Olson to Herb Kenney
August 1969

Shout to protect

Gloucester as the Last Polis

"The migratory act
of man ended
in Gloucester"

said O, to Herb Kenny in
late August 1969

"Because Gloucester began this continent….
So that the last polis or city
is Gloucester, see. Therefore I think that in a sense
man now is either going to rediscover the earth
or is going to leave it, whichever way you read it.
Then Gloucester
      becomes the flower
           in the pure Buddhist sense of
                being the place to be picked….

The 'Fire Sermon,' the truth, the truth, the truth figure."

polis is
eyes

The Maximus Poems, IV, V, VI
Volume II, 1968

Then into '69

Miriam and I had planned to come for a visit to Gloucester
        in July '69
             but were low on cash
                  so postponed it

        Olson attended Kate's high school graduation
                      from Cambridge School in June
        She was 17 and was to enter Sarah Lawrence in Sept

    Sept '69
        O arranged to meet up with Charles Boer
            his former student at Buffalo
                now teaching at the University of Connecticut

        Boer visited Olson in Gloucester
        and found that the reverse was out
            in O's Beach Wagon
        when he drove forth
                for sandwiches

Boer: "I was visiting here & I had to borrow his Beach Wagon which had no reverse on it. I went out to get some sandwiches
—all of a sudden I discovered there was no reverse....
I came back & I said
 'There is no reverse on your car'

and he looked at me as if there should be no reverse on any car & said:

 'Let me tell you something—
 Never get yourself in a situation
 where you have to go backward.'"

Then he went to Boer's house in Mansfield, Conn
staying a couple of weeks

O seemed determined to reside with Boer

Boer arranged a teaching position in the English Department
    as a Visiting Professor

& O finally began took a room at a inn near the school
that would give him 24-hour room service

    & held a series of graduate seminars
        which lasted for eight weeks

& then on October 21
came the shocking news
    of the sudden death
        of Jack Kerouac

which brought quick memories
from Charles
    about a visit from Jack back in '68

Olson & Kerouac

In late October '68 there was a surprise visit
    from Jack Kerouac
    who showed up
    at 28 Fort Square in Gloucester
    in a black limousine from Lowell
    driven by his brothers-in-law

    Tom Clark describes it concisely:
"The erstwhile King of the Beats hailed Olson
with diplomatic camaraderie, but passed out drunk
before the poet could even crank up a decent
monologue— the encroachment of cold weather
and early darkness narrowed life at the Fort
down to an anchoritic condition
    of solitude all too familiar to Olson
            from the past few winters."

    It was a Sunday evening.

Then a year later almost exactly, October 21, 1969
Jack was watching the "Galloping Gourmet"
TV show in the morning, making notes in a pad

    & eating some tuna from a can
            when the blood from a burst
            vein bubbled from his throat
            & he passed from earth

It was the second anniversary of the
Exorcism of the Pentagon.

That same day in October of '69
Allen Ginsberg was just about to leave for a
poetry tour beginning with Yale
            & then a teach-in about Vietnam
                      at Columbia U

He was at his farm in Cherry Valley—
Gregory Corso
    had come for a visit

That evening the phone rang
        Gregory answered,
            it was the writer Al Aronowitz

    He turned to Ginsberg—

"Al! Jack died."

Early the next morning
Ginsberg and Corso
    walked through the early snow
    to the woods up the hill
        & carved Jack's name
            in a tree

    in his book "Charles Olson in Connecticut"
    Charles Boer writes about the time
    that Olson learned of the passing of Jack:

Boer notes that Olson
was "startled that he had died so young."

Olson thought about going to the funeral
but couldn't determine whether he'd be buried
in Massachusetts or Florida

He told Boer about Kerouac's
showing up at 28 Fort Square in Gloucester
on a Sunday, it was either Oct 20 or 27, in 1968

Jack had come to the back steps of 28
shouting up to the second floor apt,
"Olson, the red carpet please!
Get out the red carpet!"

Not having any carpet, Olson
placed pages of the Sunday paper
on each step leading down the stairs

Boer commented that "Kerouac was pleased at the gesture, especially when he found, going up the stairs, that one of the pages he was walking on contained an article on him, with his picture."

—Edward Sanders
June 21, 2019 first day of summer

ink on the steps

Clarification of When Kerouac Was Driven to Gloucester in '68 to See Olson

July 12, 2019

Duncan McNaughton tells me
he had learned from Ronni Goldfarb
when Duncan and Genie visited Gloucester
in the summer of 1968
    about Kerouac's visit to Olson

(Ronni had been staying in the apartment
next door to Olson at 28 Fort Square that summer)

Duncan and Genie were in Massachusetts & decided
to visit Ronni, a former student of Duncan's

As Duncan and Genie went up the stairs at 28 Fort Square
Olson came out onto the deck and said
"Your pal was here last night."

Shortly thereafter Ronni clarified that
she was in Charles' apt when Jack and one of
Stella's brothers arrived; Ronni remained for a while.

As Duncan described it: "in the conversation that followed
Charles spoke very little if at all with Jack, but talked a lot
with Sampas. Those two had a lot to talk about, WW II stuff,

because of Olson's OWI experience involving Greece/the Balkans etc. and Sampas's military experience, evidently involving intelligence etc. per the Greek front ... he probably spoke and read demotic.

"Whether or not Jack passed out while Ronni was in the room, I don't remember her saying that. She may have."

And this: "The reason for Olson's remark to me was that Ted's Paris Review interview of Jack, Summer 1968, had come out sometime before we landed in Gloucester that day.

"I supposed, as Ronni did, that Charles was tickled that Jack had made the ride from Lowell to his place, rather than a vice versa. I think it was the only time the two met."

    Nothing about Olson
    laying down pages of the
    Gloucester Times
        on the steps
           to welcome Jack

Door & Porch of the bard 1957-1969

E.S. July 2019

Meanwhile, by November of '69 Olson's health became an issue
such as a continuing pain in the left part of his face
                    & a hurtful "earache"

so that a week after Thanksgiving
          he entered Manchester Memorial Hospital
                                        for tests

His pain increased
          & after three weeks in the hospital
                    a biopsy revealed a cancer of the liver

Olson called his daughter Kate:
"I'm here in the hospital
They don't know what's the matter with me,
      but tomorrow they are going
      to put some gold inside me
            & that will tell."

Kate drove to the hospital in Connecticut
                            to be with him

December 16
      on a roll of towels
      he created "The Secret of the Black Chrysanthemum"
      sealing it, and asking it be kept
              with him all the while he was still alive

Wanting Another Ten

"I really wanted ten years more
to look and listen and write"
      he said to a friend

  no doubt
  to "finish"
  the inexhaustible
  Maximus

  & enjoy,
  as he earlier said
  "this earthly paradise"

December 18, 1969
  Harvey brought O by ambulance
  from Manchester
    to New York Hospital

    hoping for a miracle, or a liver transplant

Kate was at his side
  when I first visited him at New York Hospital

They misplaced his dentures in the xray department

Late '69
  very early '70 he sat
holding forth
in a 12th floor solarium
 covered with a serape
   perhaps the one Jonathan Williams
   photographed him wearing
      back from the Yucatán in '51

A young women, also a patient
vowing that she was
  going to survive

O's roommate Olson told me
was a businessman

>   who checked his stocks each day

a NY bookdealer
>   showed up with a stack of O's books to sign

I visited as often as I could
One of 0's students, Susan Quasha
>   drove me from the hospital
>   in her green MG
>   to Peace Eye on Avenue A

>   I was busy lining up a book contract
>   to cover the Manson group's upcoming trials

>   & doing a lot of research on what they called
>   "The Tate-LaBianca murders"

>   A few copies of "Charles Olson— Letters for Origin,"
>   1950-1955, edited by Albert Glover
>   just published, were on hand
>   in Olson's room

>   He signed my copy:
>   "like my writing   which
>   sticks up forever
>   the writer

>   Zoe"

>   (Greek Ζoη
>   life, living)

> copies:
> they are full of social (economic) & political (cultural)
> examples, laws, & punctuations
> (more like ISH & G&C than
> HU, or, PV)
>
> Write, & keep writing even if i lag—for i am going to will some
> verse into existence (I hope!) any day now (he sd, the god-tempter!)
>
> 91

[handwritten annotation]

There was crazy talk during
                  his final days
for instance, about castration
to turn him womanward

since, as Harvey Brown said,
        women's livers
           can regenerate

Friends showed up
            from East and West
                      to say goodbye.

Then on January 10
        The O-Boat Sailed forth:

Charles said
from his hospital bed
the final Maximus poem
was to be

my wife   my car   my color   and myself

a bewildering, gnomic, Olsonic
finale
    to his readers

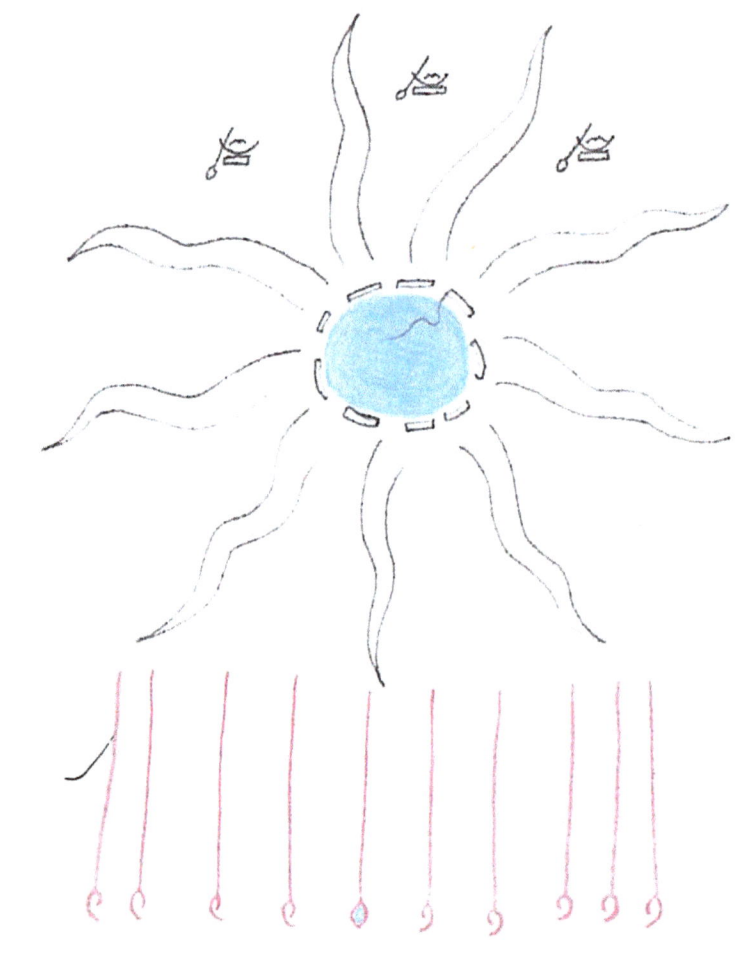

The O-Boat Departs

"I'm going to hate to leave this Earthly Paradise"

—Maximus III
197

Gaia

Polis is Eyes

The Solar Boat

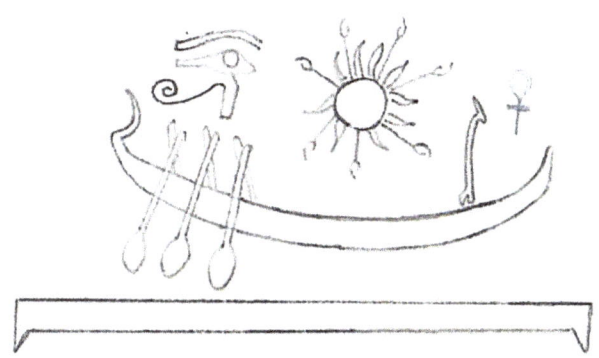

& the Lawrentian Boat

Have you built your ship of death, O have you?
O build your ship of death, for you will need it.

—D.H. Lawrence

& the Olsonian Box

I set out now
in a box upon the sea

Charles Olson
—Maximus II 203

The O-Boat

Call Me Ishmael   1947

The Post Office   1948-1975

y & x   1949

Projective Verse   1950

Letter for Melville   1951

In Cold Hell, In Thicket   1953

Maximus Poems / 1-10   1953

Mayan Letters   1954

Maximus Poems / 11-22   1956

O'Ryan 2, 4, 6, 8, 10   1958

The Distances   1960

The Maximus Poems   1960

Human Universe and Other Essays   1965-1967

Reading at Berkeley   1966

Selected Writings   1966

Maximus Poems IV, V, VI   1968-1969

The Maximus Poems   Volume Three

TROPOS

Sketch for the O-Boat
(containing his books)
that Charles Peter Olson
& I designed & built
in a lumber yard in Buffalo
in 1983 at the time of my
Olson Memorial Lectures

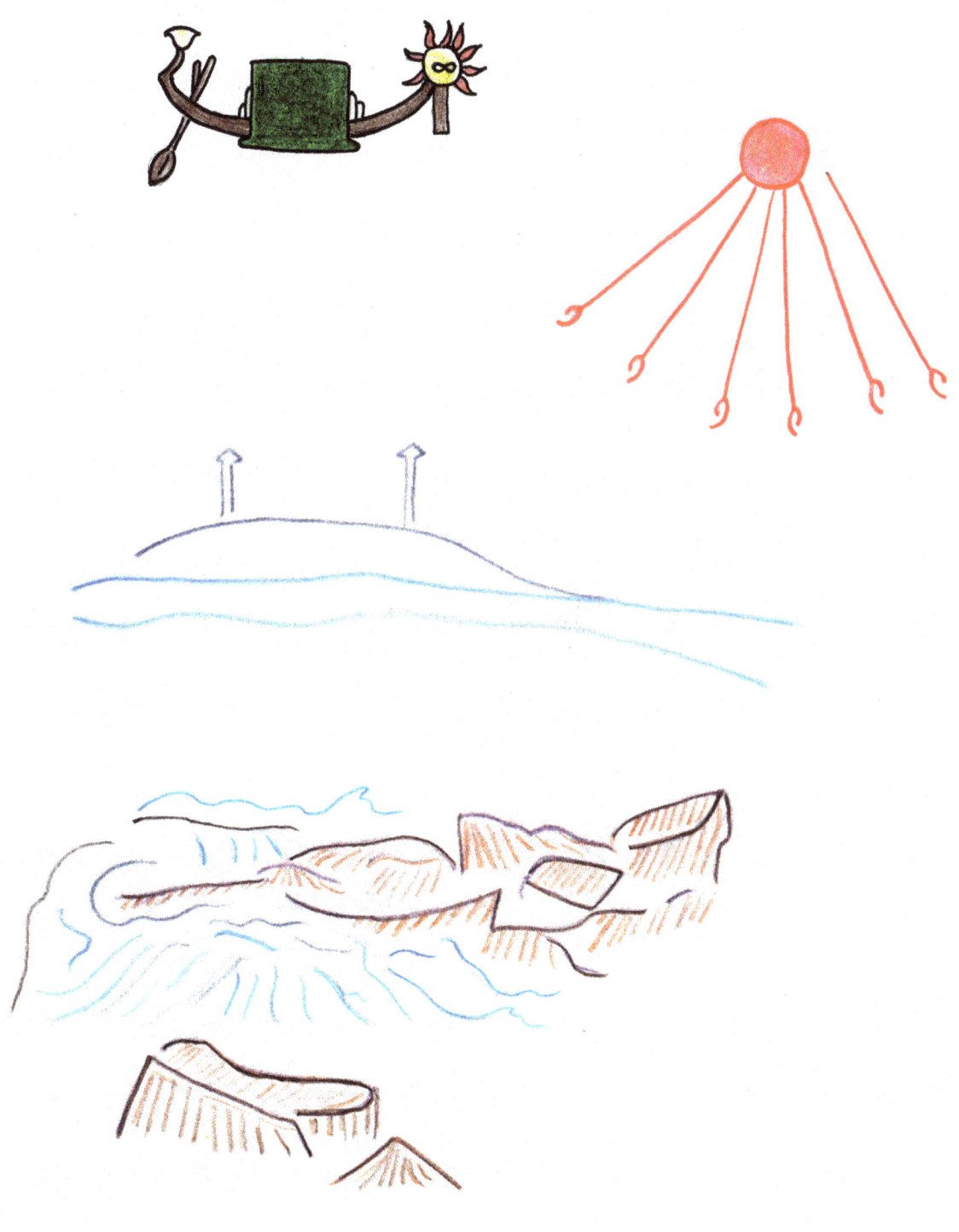

The O-Boat floats above Thacher Island & Bass Rocks

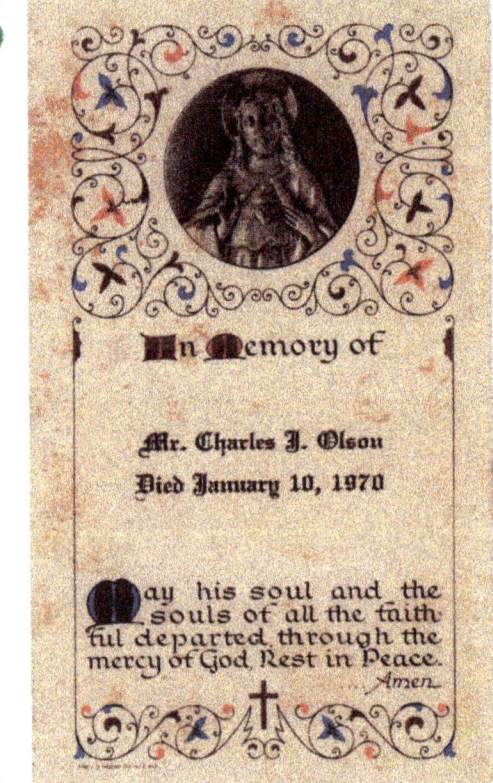

The night before the funeral
in the funeral home
he lay in a white linen suit
               in an open coffin

A sturdy white-haired guy
with a furrowed & weathered face
whom I thought
might be a local
fisherman

walked close to the quiet bard
& exclaimed
      "Charlie, you're beautiful!"

I agreed.

Stopping by
to visit
the wingéd taph

All Hail to George Butterick!

Final Maximus Volume left unfinished at his passing
      but sequenced and edited by Butterick
      and Charles Boer
           and published in 1975 —

When George Butterick
finally acquired
    Frances Boldereff's letters
        for the U Conn Olson Collection

he told me
    "Now I can write the biography"

Unfortunately
    Fate
        smashed into
           his Plans

for the enormous work
& brilliance
he brought to
    Olson's Boat!

Olson & Butterick in Gloucester
1968

168

photo: Ann Charters

Ed Sanders
2018

The "Chaos" Question

       Gerrit Lansing in Gloucester had
       called us in Woodstock
            early May, '06
       telling us about a conference,
       "Charles Olson Now," to be held at MIT on May 20

       The panelists included Peter Anastas, James Cook, Bill Corbett
       Henry Ferrini (on hand to show us an early version
            of "Polis is This: Charles Olson
                  and the Persistance of Place")
       Michael Franco, Ben Friedlander, Fanny Howe, Gerrit Lansing,
         Cris Mattison, Maureen Mclane, & Joseph Torra

It was held in a MIT lecture room
w/ math equations chalked on the boards

There were interesting new facts I learned about Olson
but when Gerrit Lansing seemed to say that he thought
Olson's main gift was "Chaos,"
I argued from the floor strongly against this at MIT

but now I'm not so convinced.

       Olson makes much
       of the birth of the gods
       section of the *Theogony*
       He begins "Maximus from Dogtown— I"

"The sea was born of the earth without sweet union of love Hesiod says

But that then she lay for heaven and she bore the thing which encloses every thing, Okeanos...."

but he is silent on the first Creation, Chaos:

                Χάος

The Theogony
beginning line 116:

Ἦ τοι μὲν πρώτιστα Χάος γένετ᾽, αὐτὰρ ἔπειτα
Γαῖ᾽ εὐρύστερνος, πάντων ἕδος ἀσθαλὲς αἰεί,
ἠδ᾽ Ἔρος, ὃς κάλλιστος ἐν ἀθανάτοισι θεοῖσι
λυσιμελής....

The first-most, Chaos, was born,
& then Earth, broad-breasted, the safe seat of all forever,
& then Eros, who is the most beautiful among
                                the Deathless Gods
limber-wanded (or as we used to say in the Midwest
in the 1950s, limber-dicked)

So, was the bard who wrote
"What does not change / is the will to change"

possessed of a deep-seated fascination w/ Chaos
as Gerrit Lansing suggested?

Hymn to O

There was a term
        of Anaximander's
inflamed my youth
        τὸ ἄπειρον

        to apeiron
        The Uncrossable
        The Boundless

& really, for years, went batty
        for to apeiron
        τὸ ἄπειρον

used to think
all the time about the Apeiron

Peace Eye, my book of verse, was part of it
Eye-Heart-Minds
        shooting the rapids
      to vanish in the Lake
        outbound to Peace Eye
that was part. To make
poems history again— that
was the sum.

Anaximander graphed the thrill of the first map, the
"perimetros," as they called it.

I had a vision
after Olson's death
of two different things

One that he walked up
to a twisted circle of rope
with the ends lashed together
where they met—

The shen-sign of Egypt
sigil Aeternitatis

and leaped through it
as if it were a tire swing

the second, that somewhere somehow
when that famous ferry's pole struck
the brass shores

        he ran into a posse of
        pre-Socratics

        who drew him
        that is to say, forthwith!

        into a delicate discourse

    There can never
        be enough of dignity
when bards
    fly flash
    to the
    shore.

I can feel you Charles
when I stare at the froth
of Gloucester's tanny rocks

You're there, next to the O-Boat,
talking with Alfred Whitehead

Anaximander is there
holding a
10-dimensional sphere

A lone Ionian column
stands on a hill
I see you O
bending at the base
writing a line upon the whiteness

You dive, again again
like a dolphin on ancient silver
through the shen-sign's ring.

Anaximander
with a perimetros
of "Earth & the Sea
    & the Sphere of the Sky"
and the endless oatmeal
of the Apeiron

Hey Charlie O Charlie
Olson has entered
the cartouche

        and this is a prayer
        that he and Anaximander
        walk down through the fields together

        o what a map they will make

        Sung:

    I set out now
    in a box upon the sea
        (final poem, Maximus II)

        So few
        have the polis
        in their eye
                (Maximus I, p. 28

    I set out now
    in a box upon the sea

I'm going to hate to leave this Earthly Paradise
                (Maximus III, p. 197

        I set out now
        in a box upon the sea

The great Ocean is Angry. It wants the Perfect Child
                (Maximus iI, 10-23/24—'61)

        I set out now
        in a box upon the sea

I am making a mappemunde. It is to include my being.
                (Maximus II, 11-12-'61)

        I set out now
        in a box upon the sea

my wife   my car my color   and   myself
                (Maximus III, p. 229)

        I set out now
        in a box upon the sea

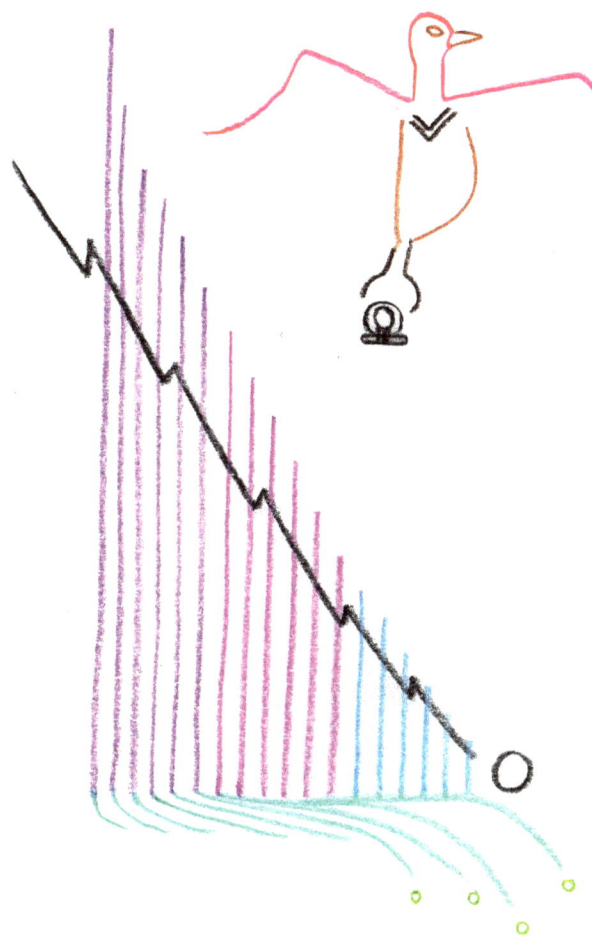

A bird
clasps
the shen-sign
symbol of ∞
which I envisioned
Charles Olson
diving through

to reach
the Other Side

"as if it were
   a tire swing"

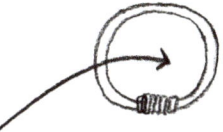

177   Edward Sanders
         January 30, 2015